INVESTIGATING DIAGNOSING &TREATING YOUR DAMP BASEMENT

Canada Mortgage and Housing Corporation (CMHC) offers a wide range of housing-related information. For details, contact your local CMHC office.

CMHC subscribes to the sustainable development theme of the federal government. Quantities of our publications are limited to market demand; updates are produced only when required; and recycled or environmentally friendly stock and environmentally safe inks are used wherever possible.

Cette publication est aussi disponible en français sous le titre :
INSPECTION, DIAGNOSTIC ET TRAITEMENT D'UN SOUS-SOL HUMIDE,
LNH 6542

Canada

CANADIAN CATALOGUING IN PUBLICATION DATA

IBI Group

Investigating, diagnosing and treating your damp basement

Issued also in French under title: Inspection, diagnostic et
traitement d'un sous-sol humide. Includes bibliographical references.
ISBN 0-662-19320-2
DSS cat. no. NH15-72/1991E

1. Basements -- Moisture -- Handbooks, manuals, etc. 2. Foundations -- Moisture --
Handbooks, manuals, etc. I. Canada Mortgage and Housing Corporation. II. Title.

TH7684 . B35I24 1992 643.5 C92-099536-5

Printed in Canada
Produced by the Public Affairs Centre, CMHC

TABLE OF CONTENTS

Investigating, Diagnosing and Treating Your Damp Basement

PREFACE

This publication is a reference document for both homeowners and homebuyers. The guide provides a quick method for diagnosing moisture problems, and identifying and deciding on the solutions to deal with these problems. This is not a "do-it-yourself guide." The guide assists in diagnosing the problems, provides options for solving these problems, and helps decide on the plan of action required.

For convenience, the guide is set up in a manner that allows its use as a reference tool. The user, therefore, does not need to read it in its entirety. The user can refer to any of the sections or parts thereof to learn about moisture in his/her home and its implications for the building and occupants; diagnose the problem by determining moisture symptoms, causes and sources; and identify and choose solutions related to any cause or source.

ACKNOWLEDGEMENT

Prepared by IBI Group with advice from J. Timusk, Department of Civil Engineering, University of Toronto.

DISCLAIMER

This guide, prepared for the Canada Mortgage and Housing Corporation, is published as a public service for the information of the citizens across Canada. The information contained in this publication represents the current state of knowledge on one of the more complex issues in housing construction and renovation. The publication cannot, however, be considered a comprehensive guide to identifying, diagnosing and solving all basement moisture problems; nor can it be considered an alternative to seeking the help of a professional.

The Corporation and the entities associated with the creation, review, and publication of this guide assume no liability for any damage, expense or injury that may be incurred or suffered as a result of the use of this guide. Furthermore, The Corporation and the entities associated with this publication, cannot guarantee or assume any liability for the effectiveness or economic benefits of any procedures described in this guide.

NOTE

All technical terms written in italics are explained in the Glossary at the end of this guide.

INTRODUCTION

HOW TO USE THIS GUIDE

Investigating, Diagnosing and Treating Your Damp Basement is intended to provide homeowners and homebuyers with guidelines to help deal with most problems relating to damp basements.

Part 1, Introduction, provides the following:

- suggestions on how to use the guide;
- a general introduction outlining the importance of moisture-related problems and a discussion of moisture as a phenomenon;
- steps in carrying out a 'housesearch' for diagnosis;
- a comment on how to choose the appropriate basement treatment.

Part 2, Basement Investigation, Diagnosis, Treatment, systematically provides information on:

- symptoms of basement moisture problems;
- possible sources and causes of these problems, and means of determining the probable sources and causes; and
- possible solutions and ranking the cost of these solutions (high, medium, low cost).

Appendices are provided to deal with more technical issues that may interest some readers:

- general information on related building materials (Appendix A) to assist do-it-yourselfers;
- glossary of technical terms (Appendix B);
- a graphic checklist and 'roadmap' indicating symptoms, sources and causes, and solutions (Appendix C) to demonstrate, at a glance, the scope of information provided; and
- selected references (Appendix D) to provide more information if desired.

INTRODUCTION

In short, this is a simple guide for householders and homebuyers which puts the problems, causes and solutions related to basement dampness in perspective. Readers wishing more detail regarding the building science and health aspects of damp basements should consult the reference section at the end of the guide.

This guide has been designed to help in a number of easy steps. These are described below and illustrated in the accompanying flow chart.

1. A. If you need more information on basement moisture problems, go to Step 2.

1. B. If you have confirmed a specific moisture problem, go directly to Step 4.

2. Read a little about moisture.

- What is moisture?
- Why should you control moisture levels in the basement?
- How does moisture affect the indoor air quality and your health?
- What is *relative humidity*?
- What is *condensation* and the *dew point*?

3. A. Read "Housesearch."

- Tips on carrying out an investigation for dampness are given in the section "Housesearch"; or

3. B. Go to Basement Moisture Flow Chart at the end of this guide if you are reasonably familiar with typical moisture problems.

4. Read descriptions of symptoms.

- See section on Symptoms in Part 2.
- Each symptom has a name and a number.

IF a symptom exists in your home, **THEN** check for the list of probable related sources and causes. (See section on Sources and Causes in Part 2 for detailed discussion.)

Look through all possible symptoms.

5. Having decided which symptoms exist in your home, read description of probable sources and causes referred to in the Symptom Section.

- See section on Sources and Causes and section on Housesearch.
- Each source and cause has a name and a number.
- **CHECK OR TEST** to make sure that the source/cause described is what is producing the symptom observed in your home.
- **IF** a source/cause is one of the probable sources/causes in your home, **THEN** check the list of possible solutions. (See section on Solutions in Part 2 for detailed discussion.)
- **MAKE SURE** to check or test for each of the probable sources and causes listed under the symptom(s).

6. Choose the appropriate solution (or solutions).

- Tips on choosing a solution are given in the section "Choosing a Solution."

7. Having decided which are the probable sources and causes in your home, read about the solution(s).

- See section on Solutions.
- Each solution has a name and a number.

8. A. Fix it yourself; or

B. Hire a Professional; or

Use Basement Moisture Flow Chart Checklist, information on materials, and glossary as required and **consult** with references, if desired.

MOISTURE ASPECTS TO CONSIDER

There is no reason why residential basement space should not provide good-quality habitable space. However, basement and water leakage are not uncommon across Canada; dampness in the basement detracts from the quality of that space and can lead to moisture damage in the rest of the house.

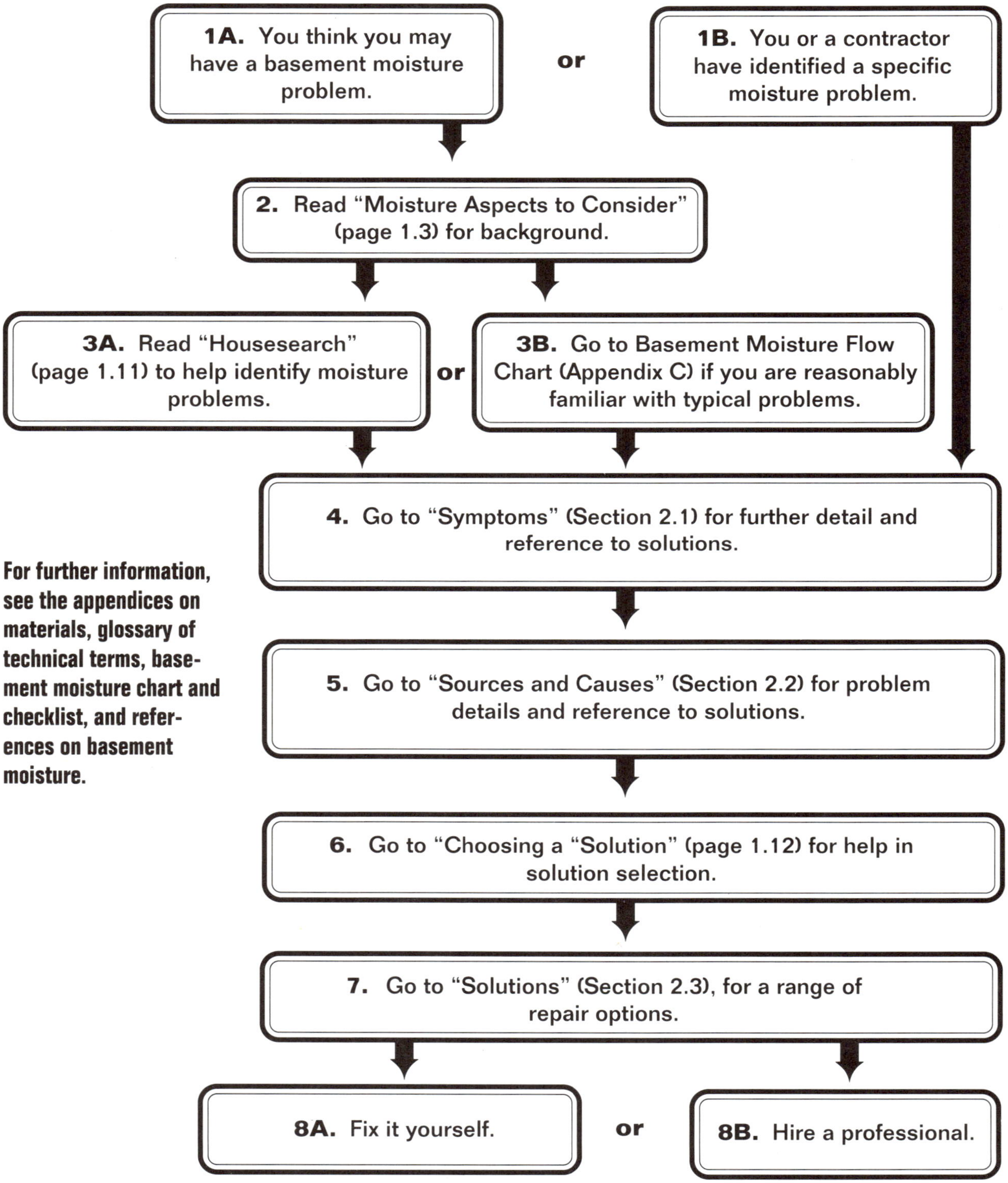

For further information, see the appendices on materials, glossary of technical terms, basement moisture chart and checklist, and references on basement moisture.

High moisture levels can lead to damage to the basement construction, finishes and household effects stored there.

A damp and musty basement is not only unpleasant; it can also adversely affect the health of the occupants. According to a recent Health and Welfare Canada survey, approximately 38 percent of Canadian homes had indications of excessive dampness or *mould*. The survey indicates that the influence of dampness and *mould* on respiratory health is "an important public health issue."

Homeowners' and homebuyers' level of awareness and concern over the quality of indoor air in the home is increasing. Since many people spend a relatively significant portion of their lives at home, they need to be assured of good air quality in their homes.

In many instances, relatively minor measures will reduce, if not resolve, moisture problems in the basement.

NOTE

All technical terms in the text which are explained in the Glossary at the end of this guide appear in italics.

What is moisture?

Moisture can be defined as dampness in the form of water vapour in the air, soil and materials, and as condensed liquid water on cool surfaces. Condensed moisture can also be in the form of ice or frost. Exterior sources of moisture around the basement are graphically shown in Figure 1.

What is liquid flow by gravity?

Liquid water flows due to the effect of gravity, which causes things (water) to run downhill. *Hydrostatic pressure* can develop and force water through openings in the basement walls or floor. High *hydrostatic pressure* can be caused by snowmelt water or a high *water table.*

What is capillary?

Capillary is the movement of water which is wicked by fine pores (due to surface tension forces) in soil, concrete, brick, mortar, wood and other materials. It moves in any direction through these materials, but has a maximum upwards (vertical) rise above the source of liquid

FIGURE 1

EXTERIOR SOURCE OF MOISTURE AROUND BASEMENT

water that is dependent on pore size. In trees, it helps transport water all the way to the top leaves.

What is water vapour and how is it transported?

When liquid water evaporates it becomes part of the air. The amount of water vapour (moisture) that air can hold before it becomes saturated (i.e., a condition where the air is holding, at a certain temperature, all of the moisture that it can) depends on the temperature of the air. The warmer the air, the more moisture it can hold. Water vapour can also travel by convection air transport (i.e., carried along with air currents moving from one location to another, through cracks and openings in walls, floors and ceilings).

Why should you control moisture levels in the basement?

- Dampness leads to an increase in the moisture content of materials and, in organic materials, can cause *mould*, rot and damage.
- Damp basements can acquire an unpleasant odour because of chemicals given off when *mould* growth rot occurs (although some rot can occur without producing this characteristic musty odour). The chemicals and *mould* spores of rot can result in a health hazard.
- Leaky or damp basements supply moisture to the rest of the house.
- High levels of moisture lead to excessive window *condensation* during winter, and to *condensation* on exterior wall and floor surfaces, especially in summer.

How does moisture affect your home's indoor air quality and your health?

- Poor *ventilation* leads to higher concentrations of water vapour and other pollutants.
- Moisture supports the growth of fungi (*mould* and *mildew*) which in turn pollute the air and cause odours and allergies.
- High moisture levels can lead to increased respiratory infections in children and adults, according to a recent Health and Welfare Canada survey on the influence of home dampness and *mould* on respiratory health.
- Chemical emissions from certain building materials and finishes increase with increased moisture levels.

What is relative humidity?

- The amount of water vapour that air can hold depends on the air temperature. Warm air can hold more water vapour than cooler air. (See Figure 2.)
- *Relative humidity* indicates the percentage of moisture at saturation that the air holds. It is "relative" to saturation at a specified temperature.

  For example, at 20°C and 50% *relative humidity*, the moisture content (measured as the weight of water in air) of air is twice that of air at 10°C and 50% *relative humidity*. (See Figure 3.)

FIGURE 2

AS TEMPERATURE INCREASES, THE AMOUNT OF MOISTURE THE AIR CAN HOLD INCREASES (APPROXIMATELY DOUBLING FOR EACH 10°C RISE IN TEMPERATURE).

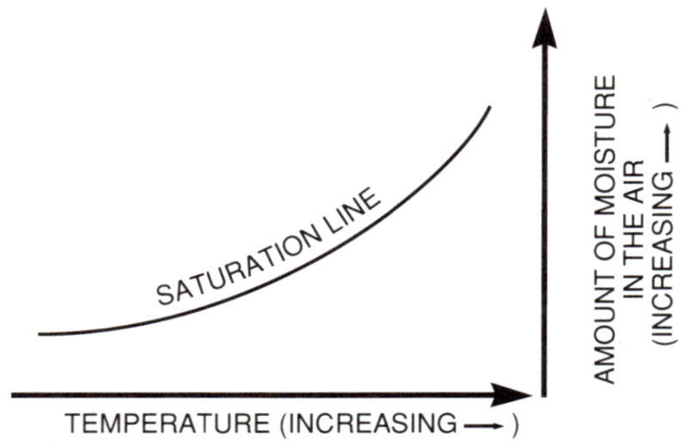

FIGURE 3

RELATIVE HUMIDITY INDICATES THE PERCENTAGE OF MOISTURE AT SATURATION THAT THE AIR HOLDS.

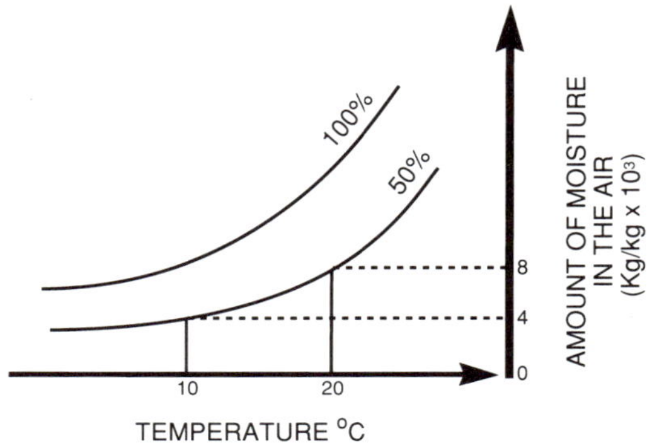

FIGURE 4

COOLING BEYOND SATURATION LEADS TO CONDENSATION.

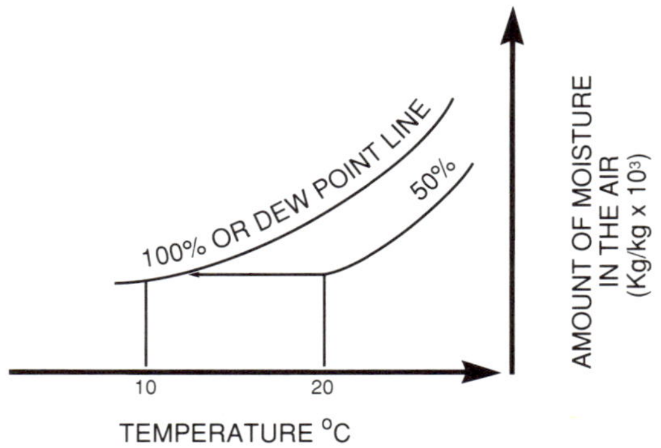

FIGURE 5

CONDITIONS FAVOURABLE FOR THE GROWTH OF MOULD MILDEW AND ROT OF WOOD.

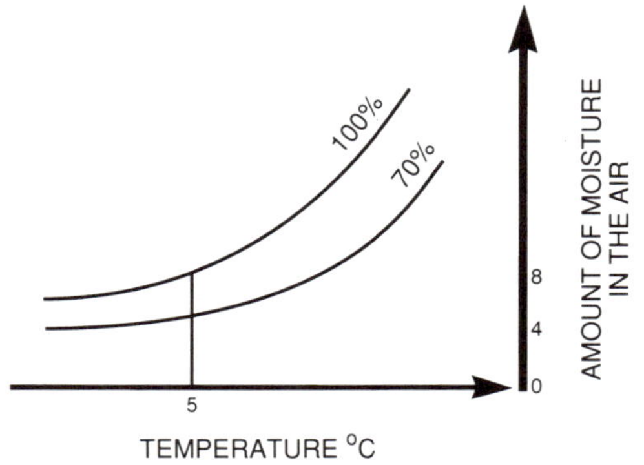

- If air at 20°C and 50% *relative humidity* is cooled to slightly below 10°C, its *relative humidity* reaches 100%, or saturation. On further cooling, moisture will condense from the air. An example of this effect is the familiar dew on grass and mist on window panes. (See Figure 4.) Frost is an example of dew that forms at below-freezing temperatures. Fog in the air is simply dew on dust particles floating in the air.
- At greater than 70% *relative humidity* and above 5°C, conditions are favourable for the growth of *mould, mildew* and the rot of wood. (See Figure 5.)
- The best range of *relative humidity* for health as well as comfort is 40% to 50%. This may, however, be too high for the type of houses we build. This is because cool surfaces on the inside of our houses (such as window panes) may produce continual *condensation* with air at higher levels of *relative humidity.*
- Indoor *relative humidity* levels can be approximated by observation of window *condensation* in the home. For example, if your home is equipped with double-glazed windows (with open curtains and a normal depth window well) and you observe persistent *condensation* when outside temperatures are -10°C (at a house temperature of 21°C), then your home's *relative humidity* is about 40%. (See Figure 6.)

What is condensation and the dew point?

- The terms saturation, 100% *relative humidity* and *dew point* mean the same thing. They refer to that unique condition where the air is holding all of the moisture it can. *Condensation* occurs when surfaces are cooler than the *dew point* temperature.
- When moisture is added to the air, its *relative humidity* increases, eventually reaching saturation at 100% *relative humidity.* (See Figure 7.)
- As the air is cooled, for example by coming in contact with a cool window surface or a cool wall, the *relative humidity* increases, eventually running into the *dew point* or 100% *relative humidity* line. Cooling below this line will result in *condensation.* (See Figure 8.)

FIGURE 6

IF OUTDOOR TEMPERATURE IS -10°C, CONDENSATION OF MOIST INDOOR AIR WILL OCCUR AT ABOUT 40% RELATIVE HUMIDITY FOR A DOUBLE-GLAZED WINDOW.

(SOURCE: CMHC, VENTILATION FOR HUMIDITY CONTROL, RESEARCH REPORT, 1984)

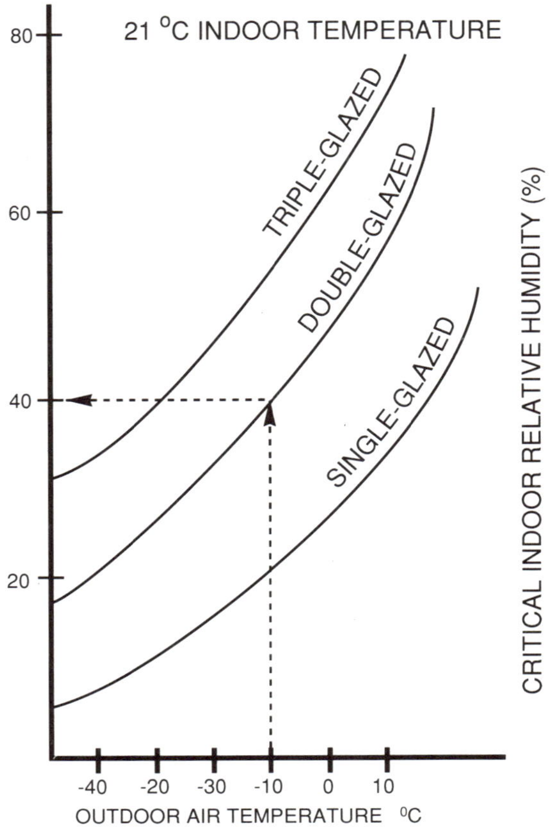

FIGURE 7

RELATIVE HUMIDITY INCREASES WITH ADDED MOISTURE, REACHING SATURATION (100%).

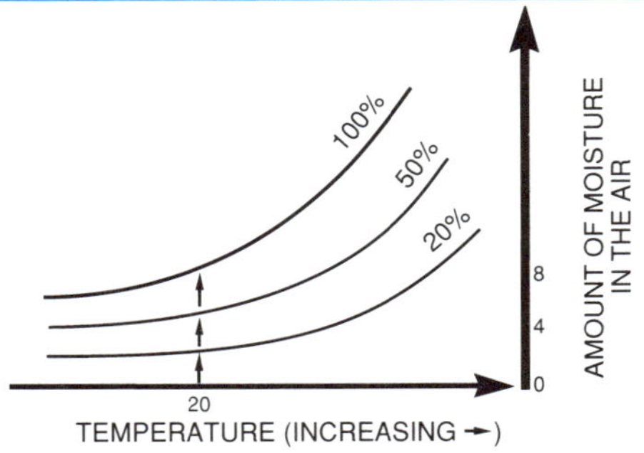

FIGURE 8

COOLING TO BELOW THE DEW POINT OR 100% RELATIVE HUMIDITY LINE RESULTS IN CONDENSATION.

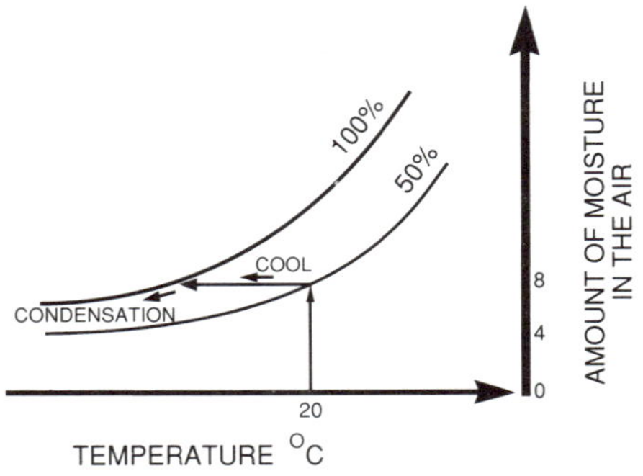

HOUSESEARCH

How to search for and diagnose moisture problems

- Most damp basement symptoms can be easily recognized. Do a thorough and systematic search. Do not just visually scan the basement, because some of the important symptoms are not easily found or recognized.
- Use your senses when you inspect the basement. Look for any symptoms in corners; between basement walls and floor slab; behind furniture, storage lockers, drapes; underneath carpets; in the ceiling space between *headers* and *joist* ends; around windows, drains and other openings; and along walls. Keep an alert nose for strong and musty odours. Since the nose adapts to smells, take a walk outside and return quickly to troubled areas to confirm the problem.
- Having identified the symptoms, start looking for the sources and causes of each of these symptoms. Again, be thorough and systematic in your search. Start looking for the source and cause at the location of the symptom, then move away from that location in a systematic manner if the cause is not close to the location.
- Check the interior basement area thoroughly, then check the exterior house perimeter. Do any testing for sources and causes as described in the Section "Sources and Causes."
- Try to find the source or cause and determine whether it is seasonal, periodic or permanent.
- Use the flow chart and checklist (Appendix C) to make sure you have covered all probable sources and causes. Fill out a checklist form for symptoms. You may want to indicate items such as location of symptoms (you can also take photographs which you can show to an engineer or contractor), the time of year the symptoms occur and their history. Indicate the probable sources and causes of this symptom in your home. (The location, time of year and history can also be indicated.) List possible solutions, their advantages and disadvantages in your case, and their cost ranking (low, medium, high cost). If you do the repair work yourself, this information will be helpful in planning the work. If you hire a professional, this information can assist in any discussion with that professional.

CHOOSING A SOLUTION

What is the "usual solution"

- Try the no-cost/low-cost quick fixes.
- Control occupant moisture sources. This is usually an inexpensive and easy thing to do, but may require lifestyle modifications that you may not wish to continue.
- If the control of occupant moisture sources does not solve the problem, make any necessary adjustment to the *ventilation;* and in summer install a dehumidifier - few Canadian homes get by without one.
- Choose the easy-to-do, low-cost solution that addresses the most critical problems.
- After rain or snowmelt, check grading, then flush the *weeping tile* with a garden hose to ensure that it is draining freely or confirm that it results in indoor moisture problems. Redirect the *downspout* away from the house if leakage is associated with rain.
- If the problem persists, implement feasible structural solutions.

What other considerations might affect your decision?

- Can you fix it yourself?
- Is it safe to fix it yourself? Are you aware of safety considerations?
- Are there other important benefits to the proposed remedial action?
- Is the cost within your budget?
- Is the solution cost-effective over the long term (taking all benefits into account)?
- Are there any physical restrictions making the solution impractical or impossible to implement (i.e., can you access the area, dig a trench, use your neighbor's lot)?
- Is a building permit required? Municipal building departments can help in this regard.
- Is professional advice or help (engineer, architect, builder/contractor) required?
- Can walls be excavated without caving in? Check trenching by-laws.

2.1 SYMPTOMS

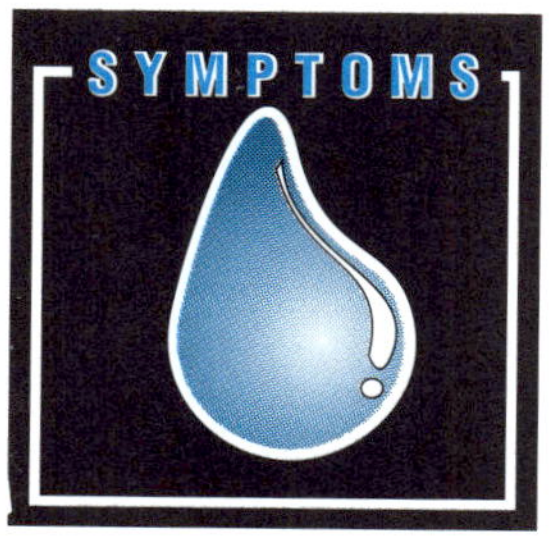

2.1 SYMPTOMS

This section describes each of the main symptoms likely to be found in a house with a damp basement. The description of each symptom is followed by a list of probable sources and causes. Each source and cause has a number (which is presented in Section 2.2). Sources and causes are numbered according to the Basement Moisture Flow Chart at the end of this guide.

SYMPTOMS

SYMPTOM

1. WATER PENETRATING THROUGH BASEMENT WALLS

DESCRIPTION

- Water penetrates or leaks through cracks or openings in the basement wall construction, including through interior insulation and/or finishes. (See Figure 9.)
- Water trickles out, causing wet spots on walls and/or standing water on the adjacent floor.

SOURCE & CAUSE

LIST OF PROBABLE SOURCES AND CAUSES

1. Surface run-off due to poor grading.
2. Lack of, or defective, *eavestroughs/downspouts*.
3. Blocked drainage at base of house's exterior walls.
4. Defective or missing *footing drainage* system.
5. Improperly drained window wells.
6. Flooding of nearby stream or *drainage swale*.
7. Melting snow adjacent to *foundation walls*.
8. High *water table*.
10. Inadequately draining *backfill* around basement.

FIGURE 9

WATER PENETRATES OR LEAKS THROUGH CRACKS OR OPENINGS IN THE BASEMENT FOUNDATION WALLS AND FLOOR SLABS

(SYMPTOMS 1&2)

SYMPTOM

2. WATER PENETRATING THROUGH BASEMENT FLOOR SLAB

DESCRIPTION

Water penetrates through cracks or openings in the basement floor (such as floor drains, cracks between the floor slab and basement walls, cracks in the floor itself, or other openings in the floor slab such as those for utilities). (See Figure 9.)

LIST OF PROBABLE SOURCES AND CAUSES

4. Defective or missing *footing drainage* system.
8. High *water table*.

SYMPTOM

3. WATER SATURATING BASE OF MASONRY WALLS AND FLOOR SLAB

DESCRIPTION

- Water saturates the base of masonry basement walls and saturates the basement floor slab.

DISCUSSION

- Due to rising moisture by capillarity or wicking action, the floor slab or the basement walls may become saturated and damp if this moisture cannot evaporate to the interior at a sufficient rate. The result is damp basement walls and floor, and excessively high basement/house *relative humidity*. (See Figure 10.)

- Capillary action will not and cannot result in the deposition of a visible layer of water (shiny surface); instead the surface will look like a damp clay flower pot after watering.

LIST OF PROBABLE SOURCES AND CAUSES

4. Defective or missing *footing drainage* system. (The above symptom could be a result of missing dampproofing coatings on walls or the lack of *capillarity* breaks in the form of a layer of gravel under footing.)

8. High *water table*.

9. Defective storm drainage system.

10. Inadequately draining *backfill* around basement.

SYMPTOM

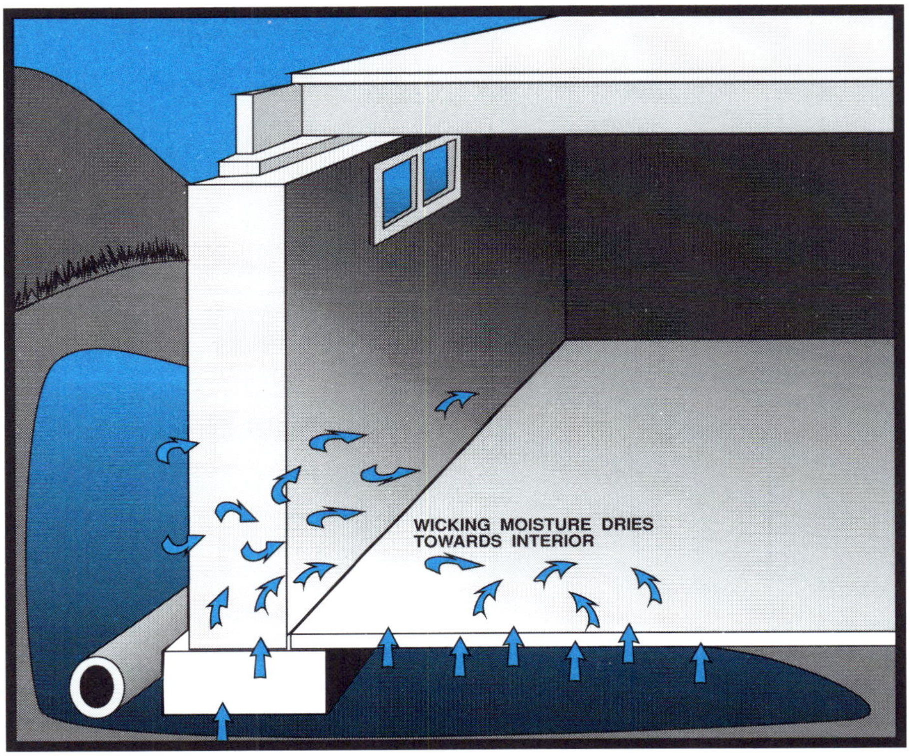

FIGURE 10

RISING MOISTURE BY WICKING (CAPILLARY) ACTION SATURATES BASE OF MASONRY WALL AND FLOOR SLAB

(SYMPTOM 3)

SYMPTOM

FIGURE 11

GENERAL DAMP FEELING AND CONDENSATION ON COLD SURFACES

(SYMPTOMS 4 & 5)

SYMPTOM

4. DAMP FEELING AND HUMID BASEMENT AIR (WINTER)

DESCRIPTION

- A general sensation of dampness, and persisting winter *condensation* on double- or triple-glazed windows, indicate high *relative humidity* levels due to interior or exterior sources. (See Figure 11.)
- Odours from household activities that take place in the basement may tend to linger. This indicates that there is insufficient *ventilation* and distribution of *ventilation* air.
- Frost and ice on cold surfaces also indicate moisture problems.

LIST OF PROBABLE SOURCES AND CAUSES

13. High indoor humidity due to occupant/internal sources (and insufficient distribution of *ventilation* air).
14. Evaporation from basement standing water.
15. Air leakage through cracks (soil gas) in walls/floor slab and from sumps and drains.
16. Water vapour *diffusion* through walls/floor.

SYMPTOMS

SYMPTOM

5. CONDENSATION ON COLD WALL, FLOOR OR OTHER SURFACES (SUMMER)

DESCRIPTION

Locations where *condensation* (or sweating of surfaces) in the basement can take place include the interior below *grade* surface of exterior basement walls, floors, cold water pipes and cold air-conditioning ducts.

DISCUSSION

The moisture content of outside warm summer air is high while basement walls, floor and air are cool and below the *dew point* of outside air. *Condensation* or "sweating" on surfaces is the result of moist outside air coming in contact with cool or cold surfaces. (See Figure 11.) (Basement walls and floors that are not insulated are in contact with cool soil on the exterior, resulting in a surface temperature which is below the *dew point* temperature for *ventilation* air.)

SOURCE & CAUSE

LIST OF PROBABLE SOURCES AND CAUSES

11. Humid outside air used for summertime *ventilation*.

12. Defective basement wall moisture and air/*vapour retarder*.

13. High indoor humidity due to occupant/internal sources.

14. Evaporation from basement standing water.

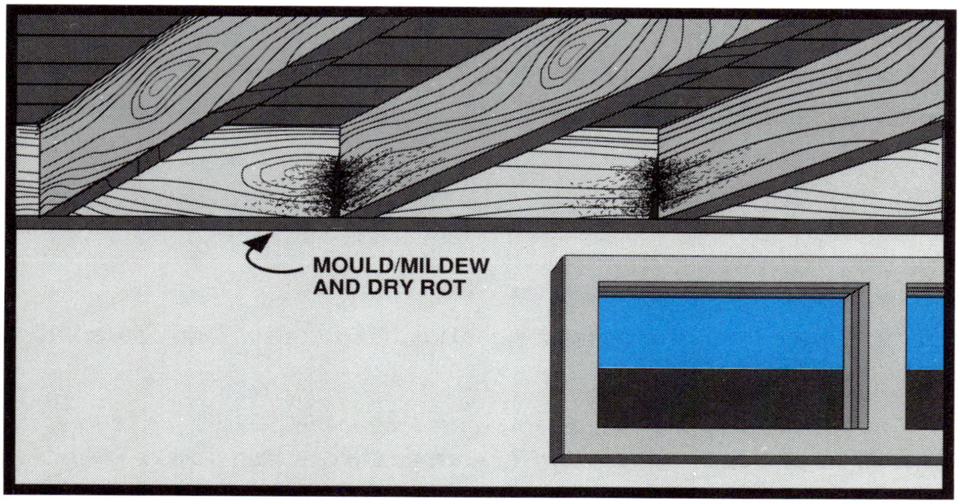

FIGURE 12

ROT AND DECAY OF WOOD HEADERS, JOISTS AND SILL PLATES

(SYMPTOM 6)

6. ROT AND DECAY OF WOOD HEADERS, JOISTS AND SILL PLATES

DESCRIPTION

- Wood *decay fungi* include *mould*, *mildew* and *dry rot*.
- Any sign of rot or mushroom-like growths on or around *headers*, sill plates and *joist* ends indicates the onset of wood decay.

DISCUSSION

- Wood *decay fungi* not only cause visible surface staining but can cause the breaking down of wood into soft and weak sections.
- *Decay fungi* need a favourable environment to grow (temperatures above 5°C and *relative humidity* above 70%).
- Decay often starts around *headers*, sill plates and *joist* ends, and can transport water and moisture to adjacent wood. (See Figure 12.) Decay causing moisture can also pass through lime mortars and plaster.
- A lack of a *dampproofing* membrane between the wood and the damp concrete (or masonry) allows the wood to wick-up moisture and deteriorate.
- The "Pick Test" and "Tap Test" are useful in detecting wood decay. (See Figure 13.)

LIST OF PROBABLE SOURCES AND CAUSES

1. Surface run-off due to poor grading.
2. Lack of, or defective, *eavestroughs/downspouts*.
3. Blocked drainage at base of house's exterior walls.
6. Flooding of nearby stream or *drainage swale*.
7. Melting snow adjacent to *foundation* walls.
13. High indoor humidity due to occupant/internal sources.
15. Air leakage through cracks (soil gas) in walls/floor slab and from sump and drains.

Note that any other sources and causes resulting in high basement *relative humidity* can result in the above symptom.

SYMPTOM

7. ODOUR, MOULD AND MILDEW

DESCRIPTION

- Musty basement odours and mouldy smells, especially during summer, indicate fungi growth in the form of *mould* and *mildew*.
- Visible *mould* and *mildew* on walls and surfaces are often in the form of white, orange, green, brown or black stains.
- Certain growths are papery with vine-like strands and often have a dirty white or yellowish colour. These can exist on damp masonry surfaces, under carpets or on framing between subfloors.
- Another indication of the existence of *mould* and *mildew* is allergic responses such as coughing, sneezing, congestion, runny eyes and nose, shortness of breath and other respiratory difficulties. Other indications in sensitive people include itchy skin, rashes, fainting and even palpitations.

LIST OF PROBABLE SOURCES AND CAUSES

Sources and causes 1 to 16 can be responsible for odour, *mould* and *mildew*. The householder should check the more obvious sources and causes first, starting with the easily and readily identifiable ones. The householder should also determine whether the symptom is seasonal, periodic or permanent, and then try to determine the source and cause.

SYMPTOM

8. BUCKLING OF WOOD SUBFLOOR AND LIFT-UP OF FLOOR TILES AND CARPETING

DESCRIPTION

- Wood subfloor over basement floor slab buckles and swells.
- Floor tiles lift up and their surfaces deteriorate. (See Figure 14.)
- Carpets and carpet tiles lift up and deteriorate.

LIST OF PROBABLE SOURCES AND CAUSES

4. Defective or missing *footing drainage* system.
8. High *water table*.
9. Defective storm drainage system.
12. Defective basement wall moisture and air/*vapour retarder* (moisture seeping from behind finished wall to below subfloor or floor finishes).
15. Air leakage through cracks (soil gas) in walls/floor slab and from sumps and drains.
16. Water vapour *diffusion* through walls/floor.

SYMPTOM

FIGURE 13

PICK TEST TO DETECT WOOD DECAY. LONG SLIVERS WHEN WOOD IS SPLIT INDICATE SOUND WOOD; SHORT SLIVERS AND BREAKS INDICATE DECAY

TAP TEST

A SHARP AND CLEAR SOUND WHEN WOOD IS TAPPED INDICATES GOOD AND DRY WOOD; A DULL AND SOFT SOUND INDICATES WET OR DECAYING WOOD

SYMPTOM

FIGURE 14

LIFT-UP OF FLOOR TILES OR BUCKLING OF WOOD SUBFLOOR

(SYMPTOM 8)

SYMPTOMS

SYMPTOM

9. LIFT-UP OF WALLPAPER AND DETERIORATION OF WOOD FINISHES

DESCRIPTION

- Wallpaper lifts off gypsum board or other wall surface. (See Figure 15.)
- Blisters form under wallpaper.
- Wood finishes warp, cup, swell and crack when allowed to dry. (See Figure 15.)

DISCUSSION

The above symptoms indicate the existence of moisture behind the wall finishes. The source may be an exterior one or an interior one, such as inside air leaking into the finished wall cavity and out at the bottom of the wall, leaving moisture behind.

SOURCE & CAUSE

LIST OF PROBABLE SOURCES AND CAUSES

Sources and causes 1 to 16 can be responsible for this symptom. The householder should check the more obvious sources and causes first, starting with the easily and readily identifiable ones. The householder should also determine whether the symptom is seasonal, periodic or permanent, and then try to determine the source and cause.

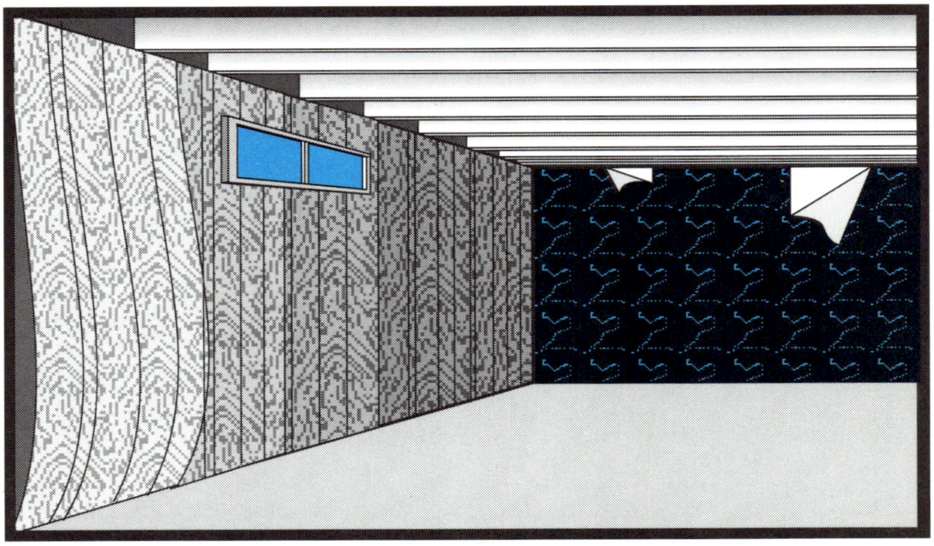

FIGURE 15

LIFT-UP OF WALL PAPER AND DEFORMATION OF WOOD FINISHES

(SYMPTOM 9)

SYMPTOM

10. DISCOLOURATION, STAINING AND TEXTURE CHANGES OF INTERIOR FINISHES AND FURNISHINGS

DESCRIPTION

- Discolouration, staining and texture change to interior finishes and furnishings indicate moisture damage. Visible signs include black or dark streaks or lines and stains.
- Paint peels, blisters or cracks, and the underlying surface is exposed between cracks or under blisters.
- Corrosion and rust occurs on metal surfaces.

LIST OF PROBABLE SOURCES AND CAUSES

Sources and causes 1 to 16 may be responsible for this symptom. The householder should check the more obvious sources and causes first, starting with the easily and readily identifiable ones. The householder should also determine whether the symptom is seasonal, periodic or permanent, and then try to determine the source and cause.

SYMPTOM

11. EFFLORESCENCE, SPALLING OR CRUMBLING OF CONCRETE AND MASONRY SURFACES

DESCRIPTION

- *Efflorescence*, i.e., white salt deposit (powdery substance) forms on masonry surfaces.
- Concrete, concrete block and brick surfaces become crumbly.
- Masonry surfaces chip and spall, and mortar joints crumble.
- Paint on masonry basement walls and floors peels off.

DISCUSSION

When the floor or walls are damp and drying towards the interior, the salts carried by the drying moisture are left on the surface as a white deposit *(efflorescence)*; accumulate below the paint (causing blistering and flaking); or accumulate in the concrete or masonry surface layers (causing crumbling and spalling).

LIST OF PROBABLE SOURCES AND CAUSES

2. Lack of, or defective, *eavestroughs/downspouts*.

3. Blocked drainage at base of house's exterior wall.

4. Defective or missing *footing drainage* system.

6. Flooding of nearby stream or *drainage swale*.

7. Melting snow adjacent to *foundation walls*.

8. High *water table*.

10. Inadequately draining *backfill* around basement.

16. Water vapour *diffusion* through walls/floors.

2.2 SOURCES AND CAUSES

2.2 SOURCES AND CAUSES

This section describes the basement moisture sources and causes identified in the previous section on symptoms. Following each description is a list of checks or tests to confirm the presence of the source and cause. This is followed by a list of one or more possible solutions to eliminate the moisture problem.

The solutions are not in order of preference or priority. Ranking remedial measures depends upon the particular basement condition and factors related to the householder as discussed in the section "Choosing a Solution." In the following section, interim or stopgap solutions are differentiated from permanent solutions and are listed under the heading "Interim Solutions."

SOURCE AND CAUSE

FIGURE 16

SURFACE RUN-OFF TOWARDS HOUSE AND WATER ACCUMULATION AROUND HOUSE PERIMETER DUE TO POOR GRADING

(SOURCE & CAUSE 1)

SOURCE AND CAUSE

1. SURFACE RUN-OFF DUE TO POOR GRADING

DESCRIPTION

If the ground surfaces around the house are flat or slope down towards the basement walls, surface run-off water from rain or melting snow will drain towards the basement walls. (See Figure 16.) This increases the possibility of water penetration and leakage, especially at the top portion of the wall through cracks and openings. The type of exterior basement-wall finish and the surface finishes around the house perimeter can also affect the possibility of leakage due to surface run-off.

CHECK/TEST

- Is basement leakage associated with rain and snowmelt?
- Does water collect around the *foundation walls*? Does it flow from other parts of the yard towards the *foundation walls*?
- Are all cracks between paved areas (i.e., driveway, porch) and *foundation walls* properly sealed?
- Is sand or gravel placed on the sloping *grade* allowing ready passage of water to below-grade levels?

POSSIBLE SOLUTION

D. Change grading around house.

INTERIM SOLUTION

B. Add dehumidifier.

SOURCE AND CAUSE

2. LACK OF, OR DEFECTIVE, EAVESTROUGHS AND DOWNSPOUTS

DESCRIPTION

- *Eavestroughs* are provided to prevent water spilling off the roof and wetting the soil next to the house, where it can splash and wet the wall or soak into the local soil, resulting in water entering the basement. (See Figure 17.)
- Failure of existing *eavestroughs* and *downspouts* is indicated by water running over the brink of the *eavestroughs*, or being discharged by (or through damaged) *downspouts* too close to the *foundation walls*.

CHECK/TEST

- Are there *eavestroughs* and at least two *downspouts* around your roof and your neighbours' roofs?
- Are the *eavestroughs* and *downspouts* plugged with leaves, rusted through or plugged with ice during winter?
- Do the *downspouts* discharge right next to the *foundation walls*?
- Does water leak through the basement wall immediately after heavy rain?

POSSIBLE SOLUTION

E. Repair, add or redirect *eavestroughs* and *downspouts*.

INTERIM SOLUTION

Add dehumidifier.

SOURCE AND CAUSE

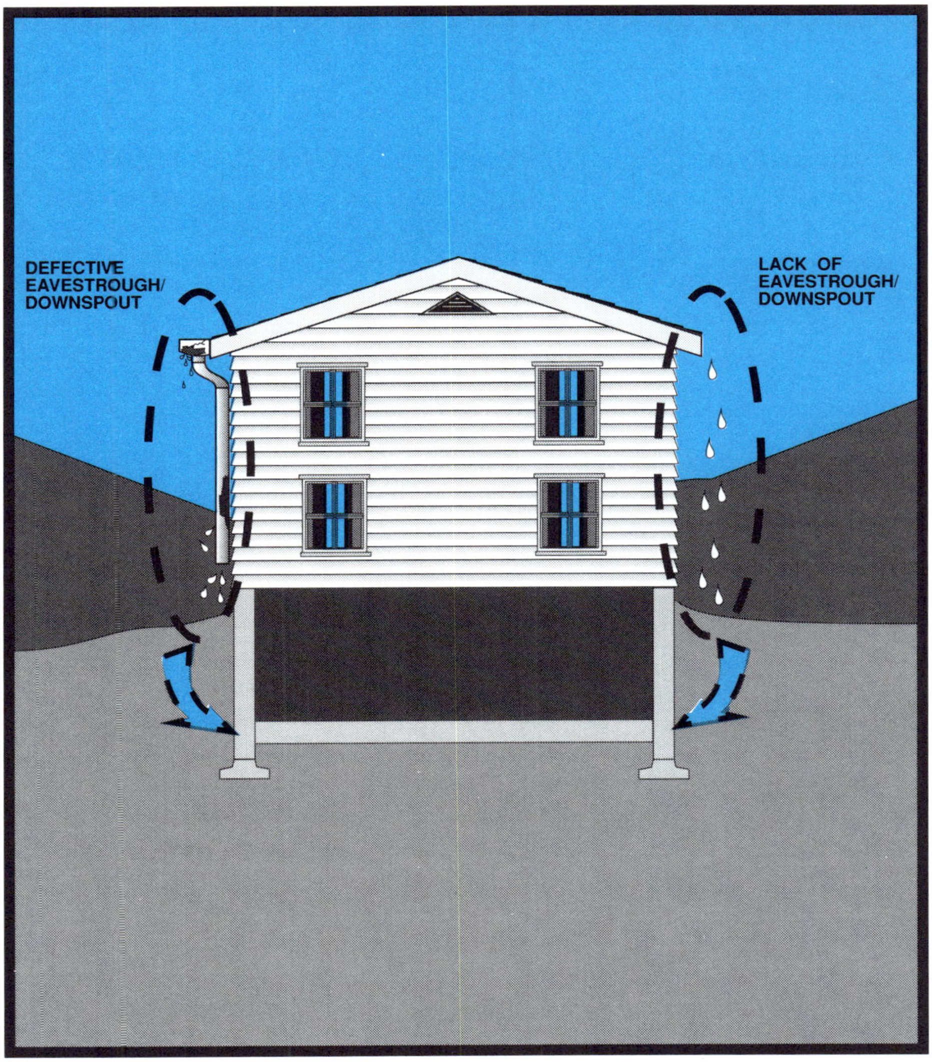

FIGURE 17

LACK OF, OR DEFECTIVE (CLOGGED), EAVESTROUGHS AND DOWNSPOUTS

(SOURCE & CAUSE 2)

SOURCE AND CAUSE

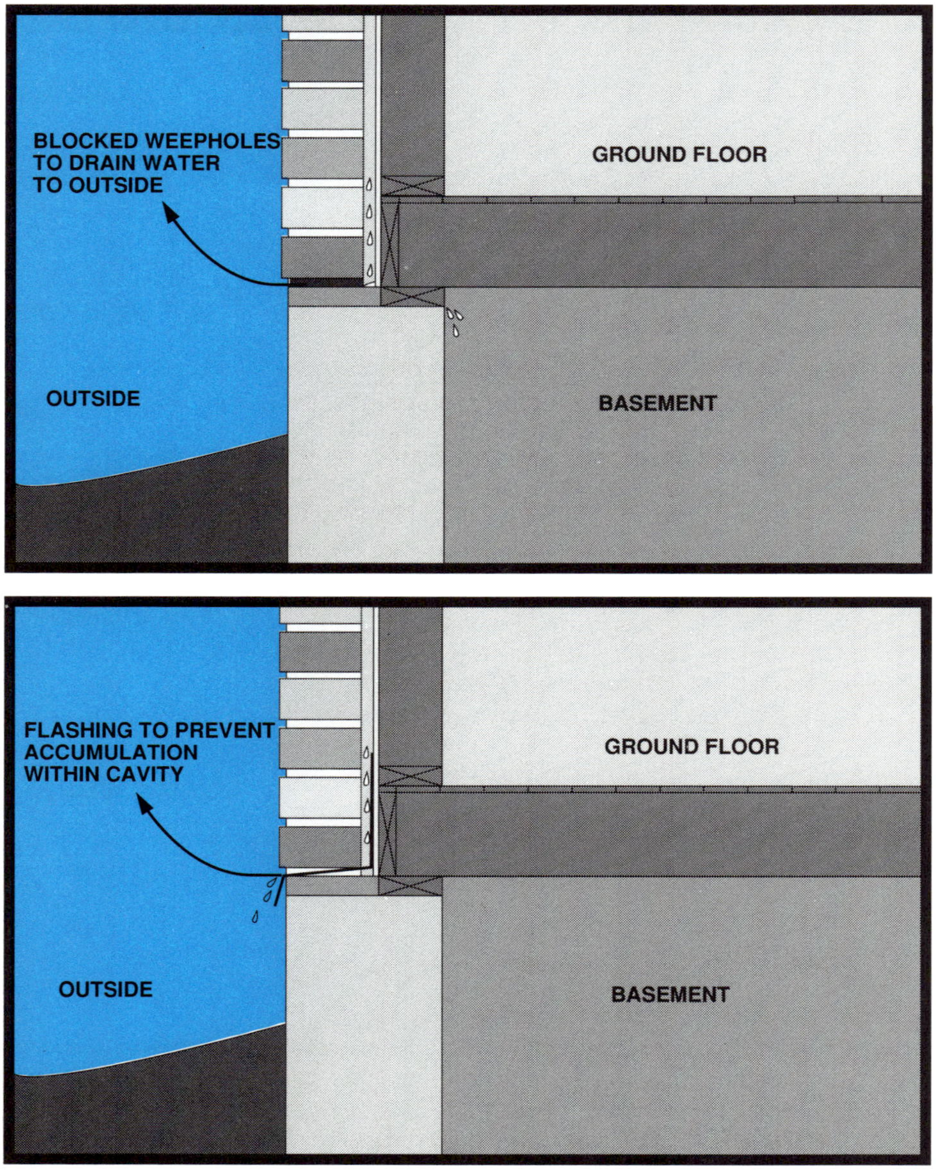

FIGURE 18

BLOCKED DRAINING OR LACK OF PROPER FLASHING AT BASE OF EXTERIOR WALL

3. BLOCKED DRAINAGE AT BASE OF HOUSE'S EXTERIOR WALL

DESCRIPTION

- Blocked drainage (weepholes in brick veneer walls) or a lack of proper *flashing* at the base of a house's exterior walls can lead to water accumulating on top of the *foundation walls* and eventually draining into the basement, instead of to the outside. (See Figure 18.)

DISCUSSION

- In an attempt at energy conservation or a misguided attempt at solving moisture problems, weepholes are sometimes sealed with caulking.
- Mortar droppings often block weepholes in brick veneer walls.

CHECK/TEST

- Are weepholes in brick walls sealed/clogged?
- Has *flashing* been provided at the base of the exterior wall?
- Is water leaking from above the *sill plate* and header area? If so, then the above is probably the cause of the problem.

POSSIBLE SOLUTION

R. Clear exterior house wall weepholes/install *flashing*.

SOURCE AND CAUSE

4. DEFECTIVE OR MISSING FOOTING DRAINAGE SYSTEM

DESCRIPTION

- *Footing drains* (weeping tiles) and a belt of gravel around the footing of basement *foundation walls* are installed to drain off all seepage water, lower the existing ground *water table* and prevent the accumulation of water around these walls.
- A non-existent, clogged or damaged *footing drainage* system can result in *hydrostatic pressure*/accumulation of water. (See Figure 19.)

CHECK/TEST

- It is usually difficult to determine whether a footing drainage system exists, particularly in an older house; and if so, whether it is clogged or in need of repair. The local municipal works department may be of some help in this regard.
- Excavate a test pit at a likely point where a storm sewer connection is made (usually at a point of entry of fresh water).
- Run a garden hose down the down pipe (if one exists) to determine whether the drainage system is clogged.

POSSIBLE SOLUTIONS

F. Retrofit (and insulate) exterior basement walls (See Solution F-2): Repair or replace *footing drainage* system.

O. Install interior *footing drain*.

INTERIM SOLUTIONS

B. Add dehumidifier (in summer).

P. Waterproof/dampproof interior basement walls.

SOURCE AND CAUSE

FIGURE 19

SILTED UP/DEFECTIVE EXISTING FOOTING DRAINS OR LACK OF FOOTING DRAIN

(SOURCE & CAUSE 4)

SOURCE AND CAUSE

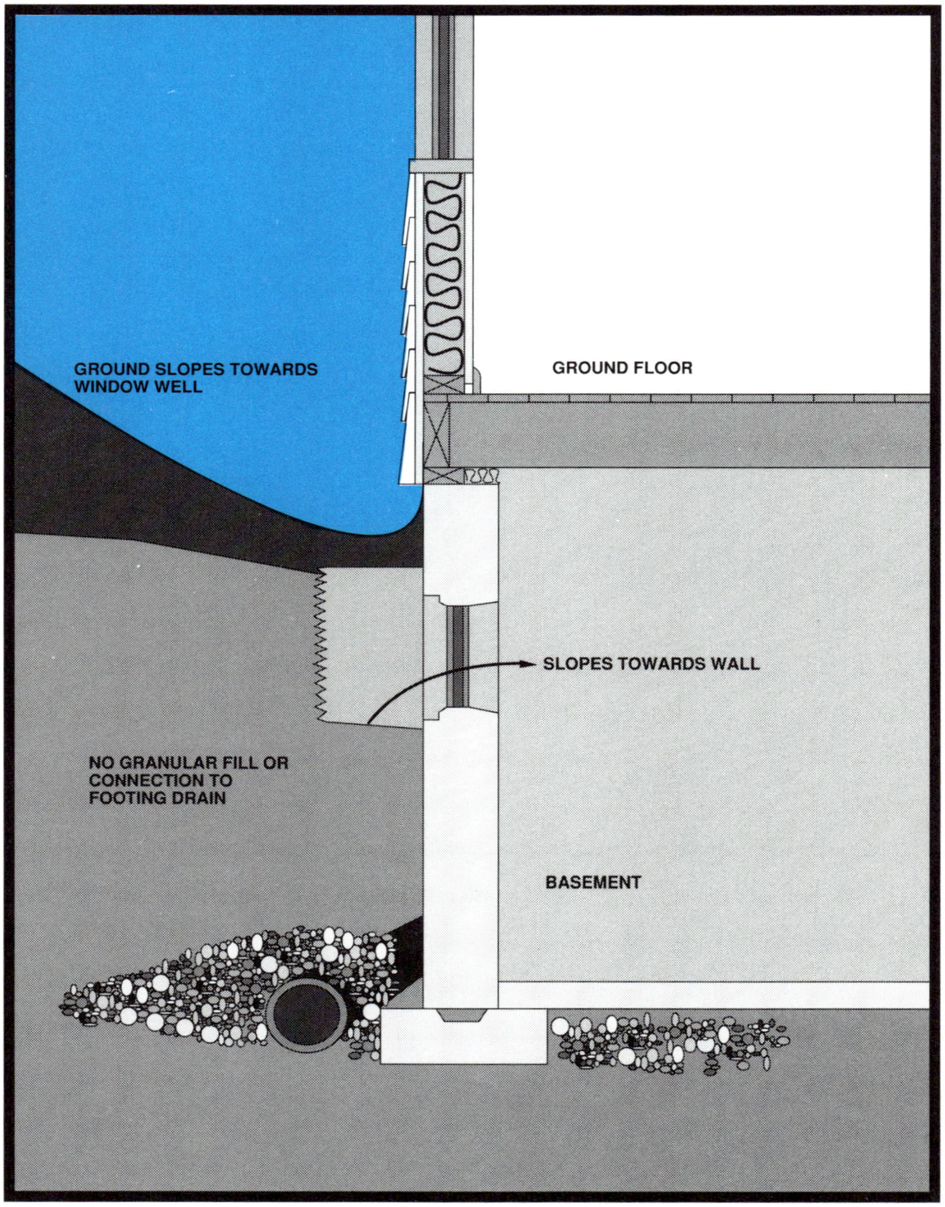

FIGURE 20

IMPROPERLY DRAINED WINDOW WELLS

(SOURCE & CAUSE 5)

5. IMPROPERLY DRAINED WINDOW WELLS

DESCRIPTION

When basement windows, or parts of basement windows, must be below *grade*, these windows are provided with window wells for maximum light and *ventilation*. If the ground adjacent to these wells does not slope away from the edge of the wells, and if the wells are not properly drained, water may accumulate in the wells, leading to possible leakage into the basement through the window or through the frame connection to the *foundation wall*. (See Figure 20.)

CHECK/TEST

Is there persistent pooling of water in the window wells, especially after snow melts and heavy rainfall?

POSSIBLE SOLUTIONS

D. Change grading around house.

N. Upgrade window wells.

SOURCE AND CAUSE

6. FLOODING OF NEARBY STREAM OR DRAINAGE SWALE

DESCRIPTION

- Flooding of the nearby stream or *drainage swale* (ditch) can overwhelm the drainage system around the house and result in water penetrating into the basement and backing up floor drains. (See Figure 21.)

CHECK/TEST

- Heavy rains may lead to leaking before flooding occurs. Check around the house for potential flooding sources.

POSSIBLE SOLUTION

D. Change grading around house.

SOURCE AND CAUSE

FIGURE 21

FLOODING OF NEARBY STREAM OR DRAINAGE SWALE CAUSES FLOODING AND WATER PENETRATION INTO BASEMENTS

(SOURCE & CAUSE 6)

SOURCE AND CAUSE

FIGURE 22

MELTING SNOW ADJACENT TO FOUNDATION WALL AND WATER ENTER THROUGH JOINTS BETWEEN PAVED/GRASSED AREA AND WALLS

(SOURCE & CAUSE 7)

7. MELTING SNOW ADJACENT TO FOUNDATION WALLS

DESCRIPTION

- Melting snow (as well as rain and surface water) adjacent to *foundation walls* can lead to water entering at the point where paved or grassed areas meet the *foundation walls*. From there it can often leak through the *foundation walls* and into the basement. (See Figure 22.)
- If the snow melts next to the wall but not further away (because of heat loss from the basement and solar reflection by the exterior walls), melt water cannot exit along normal grading slopes, but is blocked and can flood the basement or floor space.

CHECK/TEST

- Check for any gaps between paved/grassed areas and the *foundation walls*, and for any paths that might direct water from melted snow into the basement.
- Check the basement interior to determine whether water is leaking from the top portion of the walls. This may be difficult to assess if the wall is concrete block.

POSSIBLE SOLUTIONS

D. Change grading around house.

F. Retrofit and insulate exterior basement walls (using draining insulation).

INTERIM SOLUTION

C. Remove adjacent snow and provide drain path for standing water.

SOURCE AND CAUSE

8. HIGH WATER TABLE

DESCRIPTION

- A permanent, or periodic, high ground *water table*, close to the basement walls and the underside of the basement floor slab, can result in water rising through the slab or leaking through the wall. The existence of a close underground spring, periodic spring run-off and low relative elevation of the house lot can all contribute to a high ground *water table* adjacent to the house. (See Figure 23.)

CHECK/TEST

- Check for water seeping in through cracks. Cracks in basement walls, from which water may trickle or gush out, are a result of shrinkage during curing of poured concrete walls and/or foundation settling and/or soil pressure on concrete and concrete block walls.

- To check whether moisture is seeping through the basement walls and/or floor slab, fasten a sheet of plastic film (polyethylene), 300 mm x 300 mm, to an exposed interior section of wall or floor. Remove this piece in 1 to 2 days and check if moisture has condensed on the wall- or floor-side of the film. If this is the case, then the water vapour is probably entering through the wall or floor. If the moisture has condensed on the room side of the film, then the water vapour is due to air leakage through cracks or to internal/occupant sources.

- Check with building department officials in your municipality regarding the condition of the *water table* and for the possibility of underground springs in your area.

POSSIBLE SOLUTIONS

D. Change grading around house.

F. Retrofit and insulate exterior basement walls (See Solutions F-1 and F-2): Provide exterior moisture protection and repair or replace *footing drainage* system.

K. Install sump pump.

O. Install interior *footing drain*.

INTERIM SOLUTION

J. Retrofit basement floor with vapour retarder.

SOURCE AND CAUSE

FIGURE 23

HIGH GROUND WATER TABLE

(SOURCE & CAUSE 8)

SOURCE AND CAUSE

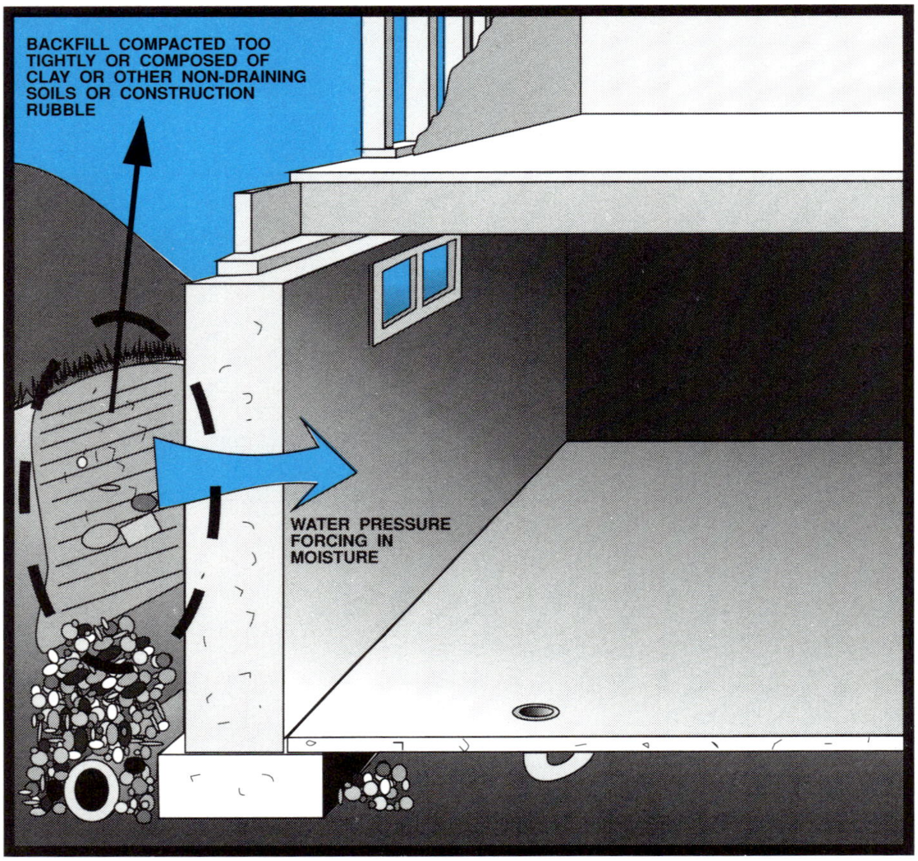

FIGURE 24

INADEQUATELY DRAINING BACKFILL AROUND BASEMENT

(SOURCE & CAUSE 10)

SOURCE AND CAUSE

9. DEFECTIVE STORM DRAINAGE SYSTEM

DESCRIPTION

- The storm drainage system (storm sewer) may be silted up, clogged or partially destroyed by roots. This reduces the effectiveness of any existing *footing drainage* around the base of the *foundation walls* and increases the water accumulation around basement walls and floors.

CHECK/TEXT

- Check for any large or older trees close to the storm sewer on your lot.
- Check with building department officials in your municipality concerning the location of the storm sewer and its condition in your area.
- Check for any back-up of floor drains or standing water in your basement after extended periods of rain or melting of snow, and ask your neighbours if they have a similar problem.

POSSIBLE SOLUTIONS

H. Repair storm drainage system.

O. Install interior *footing drain*.

K. Install sump pump.

SOURCE AND CAUSE

10. INADEQUATELY DRAINING BACKFILL AROUND BASEMENT

DESCRIPTION

- Ideally, *backfill* around basement walls should consist of free-draining, *granular material*. This allows any seeping surface or ground water to drain towards the *footing drain* (weeping tiles), relieves water pressure around the basement walls and minimizes the possibility of leakage through cracks.
- If the *backfill* is compacted too tightly or composed of clay soils, construction rubble and other non-draining materials, it becomes easily saturated with moisture and is unable to lead away water to the *footing drain*. This will create moisture problems around the basement. (See Figure 24.)

CHECK/TEST

- Check for any signs of settling or slight depressions at the surface near basement walls where rain water or melting snow often pools. This can indicate non-draining *backfill*.
- If you are not aware of the type of *backfill* around your house, you may want to dig a small pit to investigate. Make sure that there are no utility lines in that spot.

POSSIBLE SOLUTIONS

D. Change grading around house.

F. Retrofit and insulate exterior basement walls (See Solutions F-1 and F-2): Provide exterior moisture protection and repair or replace *footing drainage* system.

O. Install interior *footing drains*.

INTERIM SOLUTIONS

H. Repair storm drainage system.

L. Connect *footing drainage* to *water table* at key points.

P. Waterproof interior wall.

SOURCE AND CAUSE

11. HUMID OUTSIDE AIR USED FOR SUMMERTIME VENTILATION

DESCRIPTION

- The *dew point* temperature of outside summer air used to ventilate the basement can be above the basement wall/floor surface temperature. This results in *condensation* inside the basement on the cooler basement walls, floors and other surfaces. (See Figure 25.)

CHECK/TEST

- Are windows open during summer and hot and humid spring/fall periods?
- Check for *condensation* on walls, floors, ducts, pipes and other surfaces.
- Are basement carpets damp?
- In spring, check to see if *condensation* covers the entire wall, from top to bottom. This can indicate *condensation* from humid outside air and not from leakage.

POSSIBLE SOLUTIONS

B. Add dehumidifier (AND KEEP THE WINDOWS CLOSED).

F. Retrofit and insulate exterior basement walls.

G. Retrofit and insulate interior basement wall and retrofit air/*vapour retarder*.

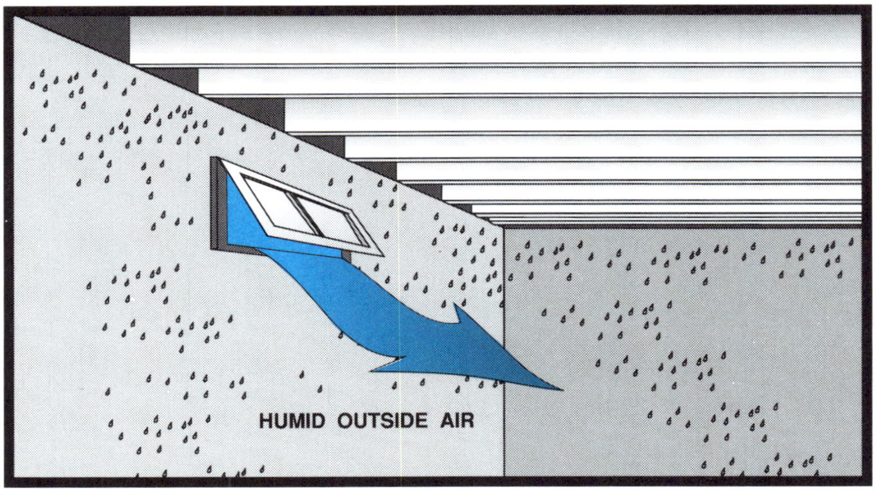

FIGURE 25

CONDENSATION DUE TO HUMID OUTSIDE AIR USED FOR VENTILATION DURING SPRING/SUMMER/FALL

(SOURCE & CAUSE 11)

SOURCE AND CAUSE

12. DEFECTIVE BASEMENT WALL MOISTURE AND AIR/VAPOUR RETARDERS

DESCRIPTION

- Due to vapour diffusion, interior basement-wall insulation normally involves placing a moisture barrier against the inside face of the basement walls, up to *grade* level. Further, a *vapour retarder* is carefully installed on the warm side of the insulated wood-frame walls (constructed against the *foundation walls*) to stop *diffusion* of moisture from the basement air. In addition, an *air barrier* (such as sealed gypsum board) is located on the room side of the insulation to prevent indoor air currents from depositing moisture in the cavity.
- Note that neither the moisture barrier against the wall nor the *vapour retarder* is capable of stopping liquid water flow, only the flow of water vapour.

CHECK TEST

CHECK/TEST

- Check to see if water appears on the floor after a spring thaw and not only after heavy summer rain.
- Rotting of wall studs may be hard to detect if the wall is finished. You may want to remove part of the finished surface of the wall.
- If the basement walls are insulated but are not finished with plywood panelling or drywall, it is possible to check for rotting wood studs, wet insulation and excessive tears in the air/*vapour retarder*, and for areas that are not properly sealed (such as electrical outlets and panels, plumbing and joist ends). (See Figure 26.)
- If the interior wall surfaces are covered, deterioration and damage to interior finishes may indicate that the air/*vapour retarder* is damaged or defective.

SOLUTIONS

POSSIBLE SOLUTIONS

G. Retrofit and (properly) insulate interior basement walls and retrofit air/*vapour retarder*.

Q. Seal and control air leaks.

SOURCE AND CAUSE

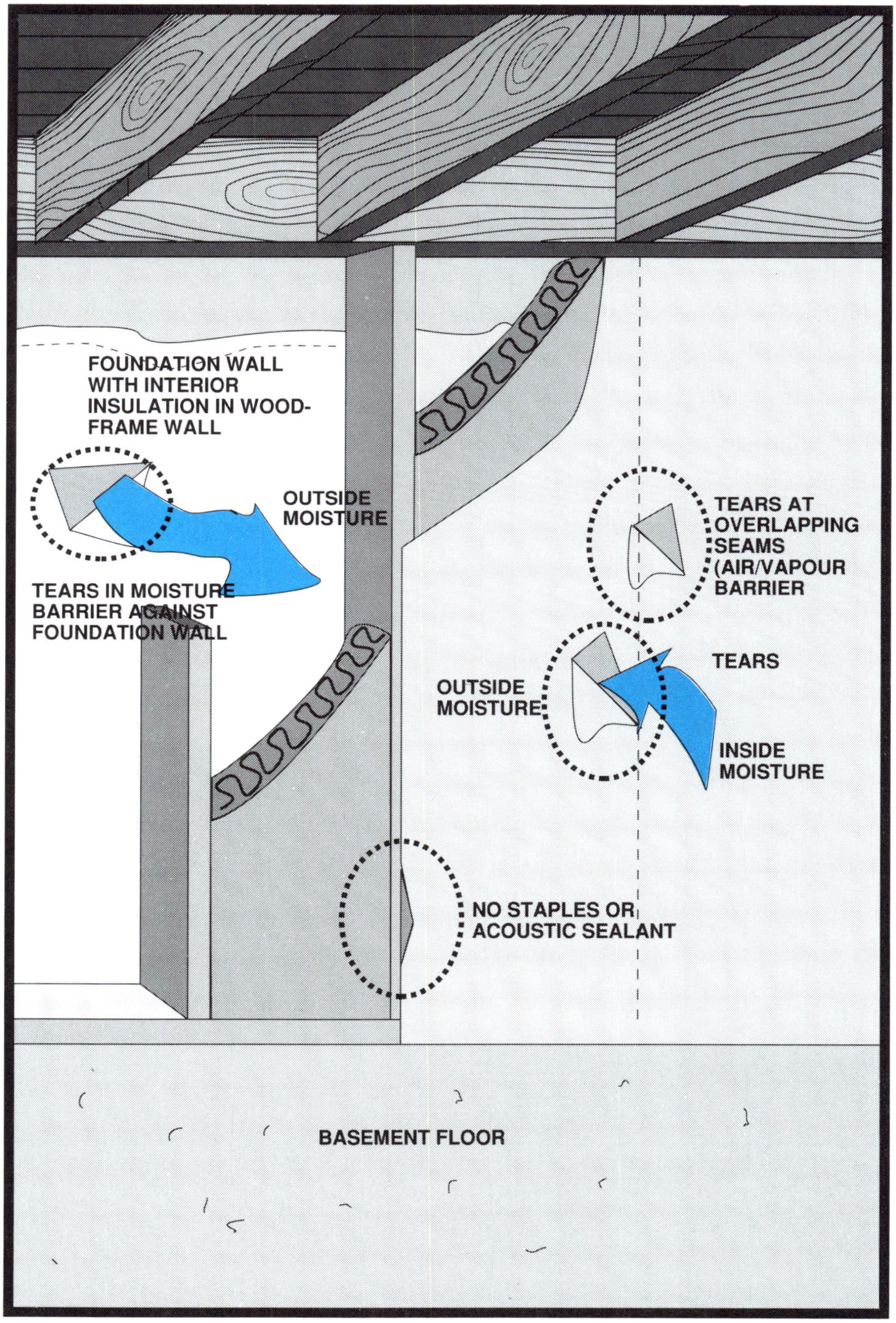

FIGURE 26

DEFECTIVE BASEMENT-WALL MOISTURE AND AIR/VAPOUR BARRIERS ALLOW INSIDE AND OUTSIDE MOISTURE TO GET INTO WALL CAVITY AND CAUSE DAMAGE

(SOURCE AND CAUSE 12)

SOURCE AND CAUSE

13. HIGH INDOOR HUMIDITY DUE TO OCCUPANT/INTERNAL SOURCES

DESCRIPTION

- Many of the inside sources of moisture-causing high *relative humidity* levels are related to occupant activities and household equipment. Moisture sources anywhere in the house (especially with a forced-air system) can cause basement moisture problems. These sources can lead to prolonged high *relative humidity* levels, causing a variety of moisture-related problems. Basement sources and causes include:
- Clothes dryer not vented to the outside.
- Defective clothes dryer vent.
- Storage of damp materials such as firewood.
- Aquariums (minor source).
- Bathing and showers in unvented basement bathrooms.
- Clothes drying on indoor line.
- Spillage of combustion gases from furnace and/or unvented burning fuel heaters.
- Humidifier in the basement or humidifying device on the furnace.
- Faulty cooling or heating systems, resulting in water leakage.
- Whirlpools, baths, hot tubs and house plants.
- Drying out of high-water-content construction materials, especially during the first year following construction completion.

CHECK/TEST

- Check basement (and then the rest of the house) for the existence of any of the above probable sources and causes.

POSSIBLE SOLUTIONS

A. Add or adjust mechanical *ventilation*.

SOURCE AND CAUSE

G. Retrofit and insulate interior basement walls and retrofit air/*vapour retarders*.

I. Remove and/or control internal/occupant sources (those listed above, including removing humidifier on furnace).

INTERIM SOLUTION

B. Add dehumidifier.

SOURCE AND CAUSE

14. EVAPORATION FROM BASEMENT STANDING WATER

DESCRIPTION

- Water vapour and high levels of *relative humidity* may be a result of evaporation from standing water within the basement.
- Sources include an open sump pit; wet floors; standing water or moisture-saturated soil in adjacent crawl spaces, such as in the lower level of a split-level house; or an indoor swimming pool.

CHECK/TEST

- Check for any of the above or other possibilities of evaporation as a result of standing water.

POSSIBLE SOLUTIONS

A. Add or adjust mechanical *ventilation*.

I. Remove or control internal/occupant sources (mainly standing water).

INTERIM SOLUTION

B. Add dehumidifier.

15. AIR LEAKAGE THROUGH CRACKS (SOIL GAS) IN WALLS/ FLOOR SLAB AND FROM SUMPS AND DRAINS

DESCRIPTION

- Air leakage through cracks in basement walls and floor slab can transport a relatively high amount of moisture.

  This air is also known as soil gas and is often at 100% *relative humidity* (saturated) at the basement-floor temperature. (See Figure 27.)

- Soil gas may contain *radon* gas (in certain locations), methane gas (near landfill sites) or other dangerous contaminants (e.g., gasoline from a leaking fuel storage tank).

CHECK/TEST

- Check for cracks in and between the walls and floor slab.
- Check for tight sealing around utility pipes.
- Make sure that floor drains and sump pits are covered and vented outdoors, and that drain traps are filled with water.
- Basements are often at a slight negative pressure, and infiltrating air can create a slight, yet detectable, draft in areas with large cracks or infiltration sources. You may use a makeshift leak detector by holding one or more incense sticks. Strong leaks will cause the smoke to dissipate and the tip of the sticks to glow. Weaker leaks will create smoke trails away from the leak.

POSSIBLE SOLUTIONS

A. Add or adjust mechanical *ventilation*. (Adjust *ventilation* system to reduce negative pressure in basement. Add more make-up air or forced-air supplies to basement.)

G. Retrofit and insulate interior basement walls and retrofit air/*vapour retarder*.

SOURCE AND CAUSE

O. Install interior *footing drain* (and vent to outdoors).

Q. Seal and control air leaks.

INTERIM SOLUTION

M. Install interior *gutter* system (to collect leakage and vent gases to outdoors).

FIGURE 27

AIR LEAKAGE THROUGH CRACKS IN BASEMENT WALLS AND FLOOR

(SOURCE & CAUSE 15)

16. WATER VAPOUR DIFFUSION THROUGH WALLS/FLOOR

DESCRIPTION

Soil gas (around footings, basement walls and below the floor slab) has a higher vapour content than basement air, especially in winter when the outdoor air is dry. This leads to a water-vapour flow from the soil diffusing into the floor slab and basement walls, and through them, to the basement interior. (See Figure 28.)

DISCUSSION

High rates of vapour *diffusion* are usually due to inadequate *dampproofing* of the walls and floor, and a lack of capillary breaks on the exterior.

Soil gas water-vapour pressure can drive vapour flow indoors if the pressure is higher than the basement vapour pressure. Soil water can also wet the *foundation wall* and basement slab surfaces so that *capillarity* can wick water to indoor surfaces. Evaporation of water from these surfaces wets the indoor air.

CHECK/TEST

To check whether water vapour is diffusing through the basement walls and/or floor slab, fasten a small, 300 mm x 300 mm, piece of plastic film (polyethylene) to an exposed interior section of the wall/floor. Remove this piece in 1 to 2 days, and check if moisture is condensed on the wall/floor side of the film. If this is the case, then water vapour is probably diffusing/wicking through the walls. Otherwise, the source of moisture may be from occupants or other internal sources.

It is often difficult to determine whether *diffusion* or *capillarity* is the major flow mechanism, and both may be at work at various depths through the wall.

POSSIBLE SOLUTIONS

F. Retrofit (and insulate) exterior basement walls (See Solution F-1): Provide exterior moisture protection.

G. Retrofit and insulate interior walls and retrofit air/*vapour retarders.*

SOURCE & CAUSE

SOURCE AND CAUSE

SOLUTIONS

INTERIM SOLUTIONS

M. Install interior *gutter* system (to collect leakage).

P. Waterproof/dampproof interior basement walls (and floor).

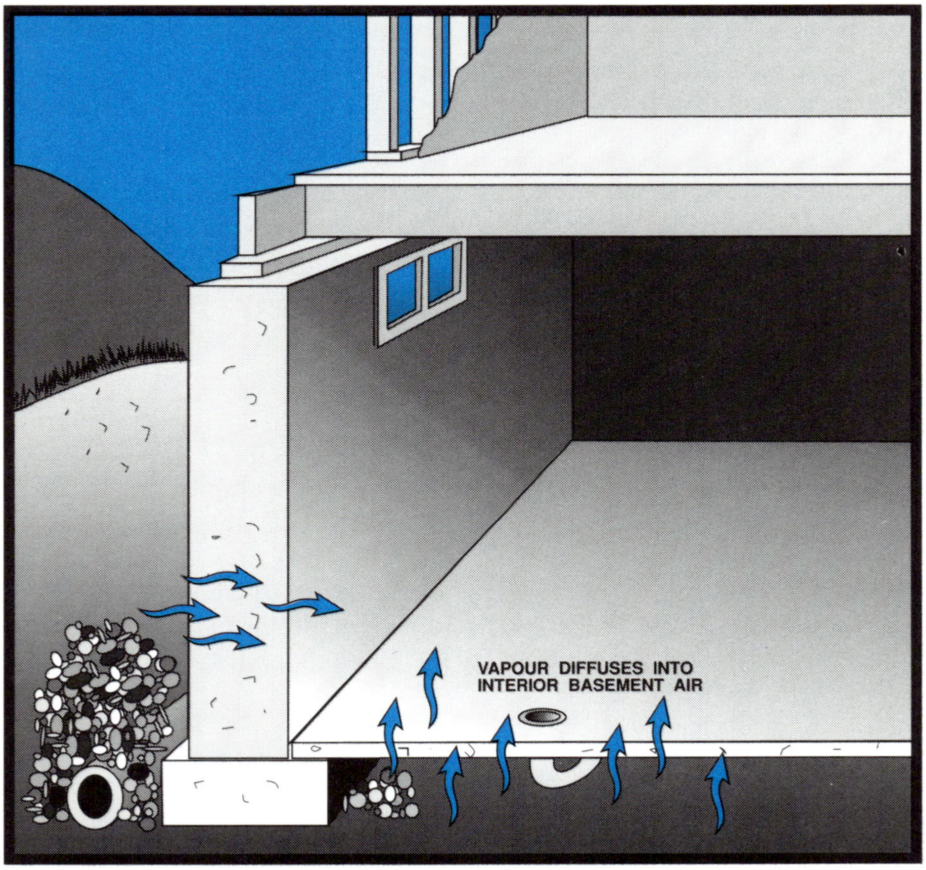

FIGURE 28

WATER VAPOUR DIFFUSION FROM SOIL SURROUNDING THE BASEMENT

(SOURCE & CAUSE 16)

2.3 SOLUTIONS

2.3 SOLUTIONS

The following solutions are described in general terms.

Note that most solutions will require professional advice. Check with a local building official and/or a contractor before attempting work that is unfamiliar or requires special equipment.

The cost of solutions may differ from one situation to another, based on the extent of the problem, its location and conditions and factors that may influence the implementation of such a solution. In general, solutions can be ranked, based on assumed conditions and average market costs for implementation. A ranking by cost of Low/Medium/High is used throughout this guide, but costs may vary depending on the problem, location, amount of householder labour used and other factors.

SOLUTION

A. ADD OR ADJUST MECHANICAL VENTILATION

DESCRIPTION

- Natural *ventilation* is not reliable in controlling moisture levels in the basement, since the moisture content and leakage intake rate of outdoor air is governed by weather and the "leakiness" of the basement/house construction.
- In summer and other hot and humid periods, you should NOT ventilate the basement with outdoor air. The basement should be dehumidified (keeping windows closed) or insulated to raise the temperature of all surfaces above the *dew point* temperature of the outside summertime air.
- Electrically heated houses lacking a chimney, often have a lower basement *ventilation* rate than houses with fuel-fired furnaces. If electrically-heated houses have moisture problems, mechanical *ventilation* may be needed.
- Heat-recovery ventilators (HRVs or air-to-air heat exchangers) and heat pump exhaust HRVs (air-change heat pumps) are suitable for mechanical *ventilation* in winter. (See Figure 29.)
- A window air conditioner can be used to condition and dehumidify the basement in summer if the basement is not already cool, compared to the rest of the house.

LOW TO MEDIUM COST

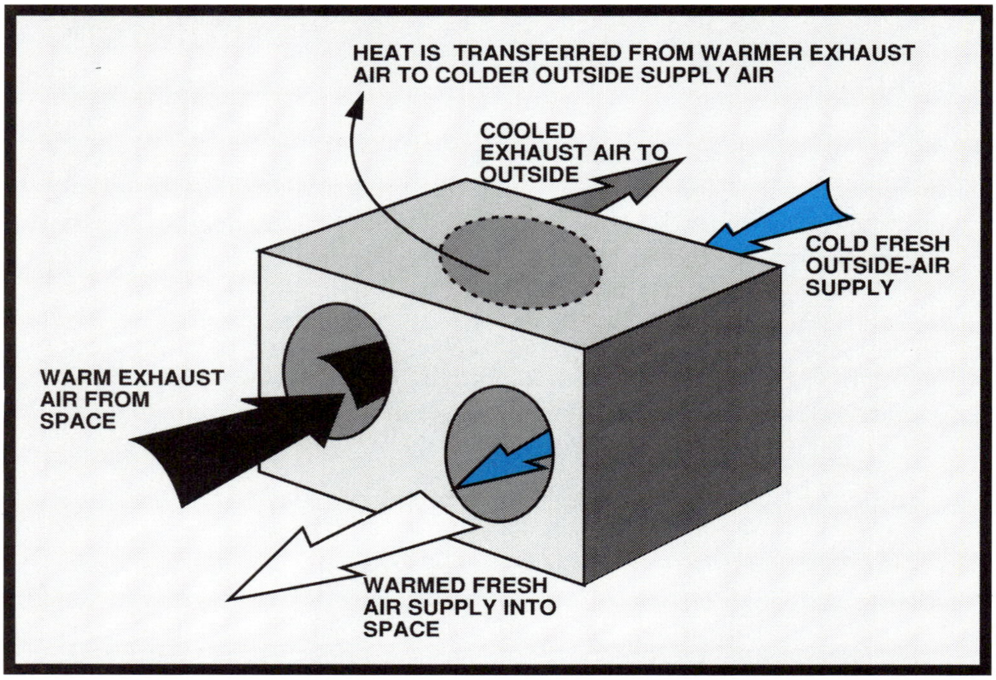

FIGURE 29a

HEAT-RECOVERY VENTILATOR OR AIR-TO-AIR HEAT EXCHANGER

(SOLUTION A)

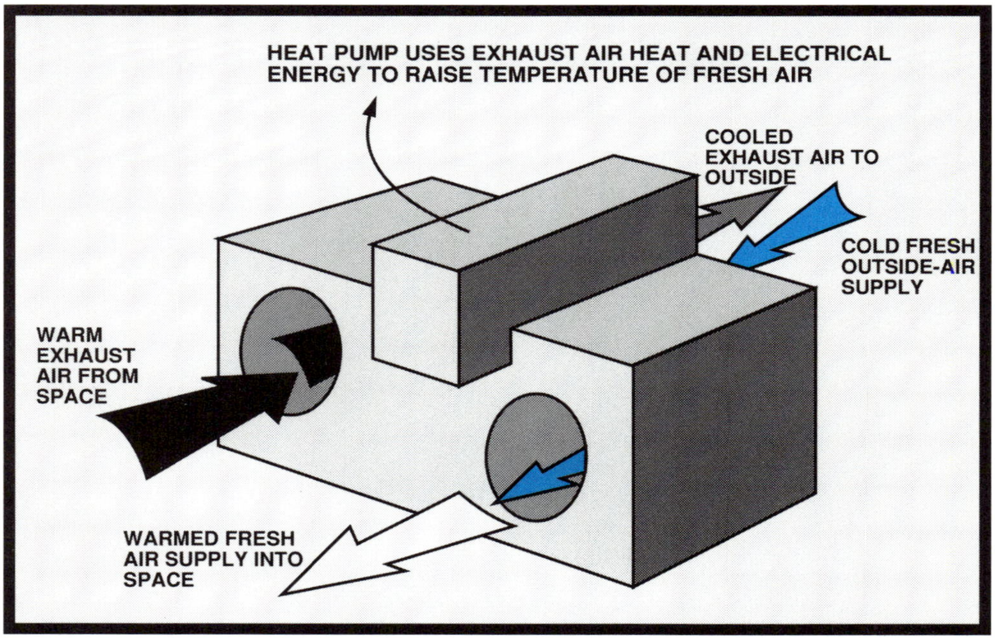

FIGURE 29b

HEAT PUMP EXHAUST HEAT-RECOVERY VENTILATIOR OR AIR-CHANGE HEAT PUMP

(SOLUTION A)

SOLUTION

B. ADD DEHUMIDIFIER

DESCRIPTION

- One way of reducing high *relative humidity* in the basement is to use a dehumidifier. This will not correct the source of the problem but can alleviate the symptoms. The use of a dehumidifier is most effective in summer or humid spring/fall periods. Basement windows should be kept closed. For good circulation, the dehumidifier should be placed in the centre of the basement.
- Chemical dehumidifiers using desiccants, such as silica gel, in containers are not practical for basements and large spaces since the chemicals may have to be replaced or dried out on a daily basis.
- Mechanical dehumidifiers used in basements are of the refrigeration type that remove moisture by drawing air over a cooling coil (condenser). Water vapour condenses on the cooling coil and drains off into a collection pan, or through a hose to the floor drain. They help heat the room, even though they cool the air, because the heat pump adds more heat to the rest of the room than the condenser does to the coil.
- Dehumidifier efficiency is rated at the ability to condense water from air at 27°C and 60% *relative humidity*. Efficiency drops at room temperatures, and there is a practical lower limit to the *relative humidity* that can be produced by a dehumidifier. During summer, one should be satisfied if basement *relative humidity* is brought down to 70%.
- The capacity of collection pans of dehumidifiers vary. The pans and the coils should be cleaned regularly to prevent the growth of *mould* and other organisms.

LOW TO MEDIUM COST

SOLUTION

C. REMOVE ADJACENT SNOW AND PROVIDE DRAIN PATH FOR STANDING WATER

DESCRIPTION

- Surface grading away from basement walls should be maintained and drainage channels provided.
- If pooling occurs due to snow melt, snow adjacent to basement walls should be removed in the spring before it melts and forms dykes which prevent drainage.
- Flower and vegetable beds should be graded away from the house perimeter to prevent accumulations of standing water. They could also be placed away from the house perimeter. (See Figure 30.)
- An electric tracer cable (used with a ground-faulted receptacle only) can be used to break through ice dams.

LOW COST

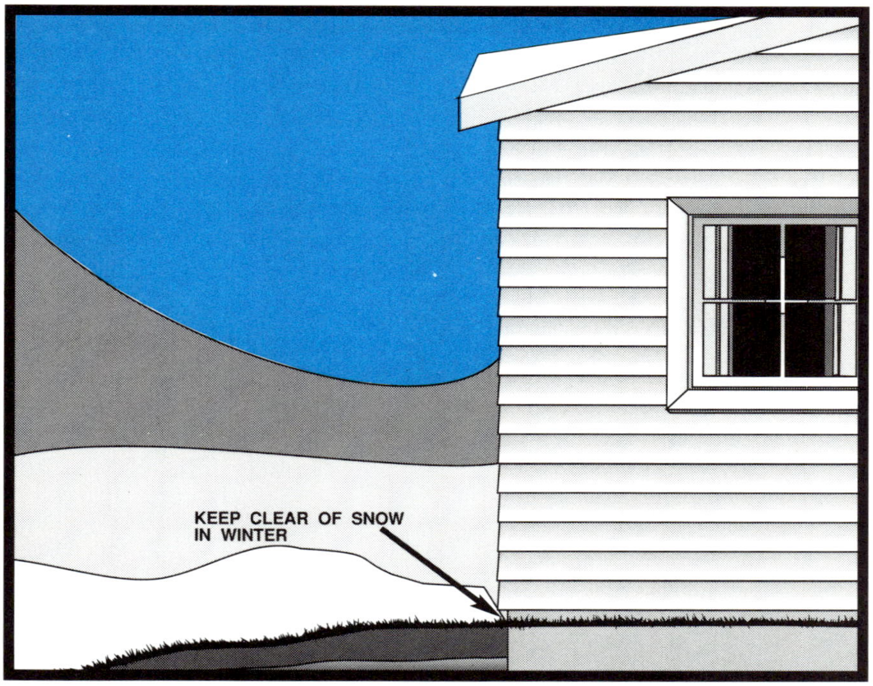

FIGURE 30

REMOVE ADJACENT SNOW AND POSSIBLE SOURCES OF STANDING WATER FROM FOUNDATION WALL (HOUSE PERIMETER)

(SOLUTION C)

D. CHANGE GRADING AROUND HOUSE

DESCRIPTION

- The *grade* around the house's basement walls should be sloped away from the house for a distance of 2.5 m to 3.5 m, wherever possible and feasible.
- A slope of 10% to 12% (1 in 10 to 1 in 8) is adequate to drain away surface water and avoid pooling.
- A layer of native top-soil, clay or bentonite placed on the slope prior to sodding can provide a relatively impervious layer. This layer reduces penetration of surface water into the *backfill* adjacent to basement walls. (See Figure 31.)
- Sloped *grade* can be paved or topped with grass.
- Sodding of a newly graded slope can prevent the washing away of the top layer of the soil.
- Surface run-off from nearby areas can be diverted with shallow swales perpendicular to the direction of the water flow.

LOW TO MEDIUM COST

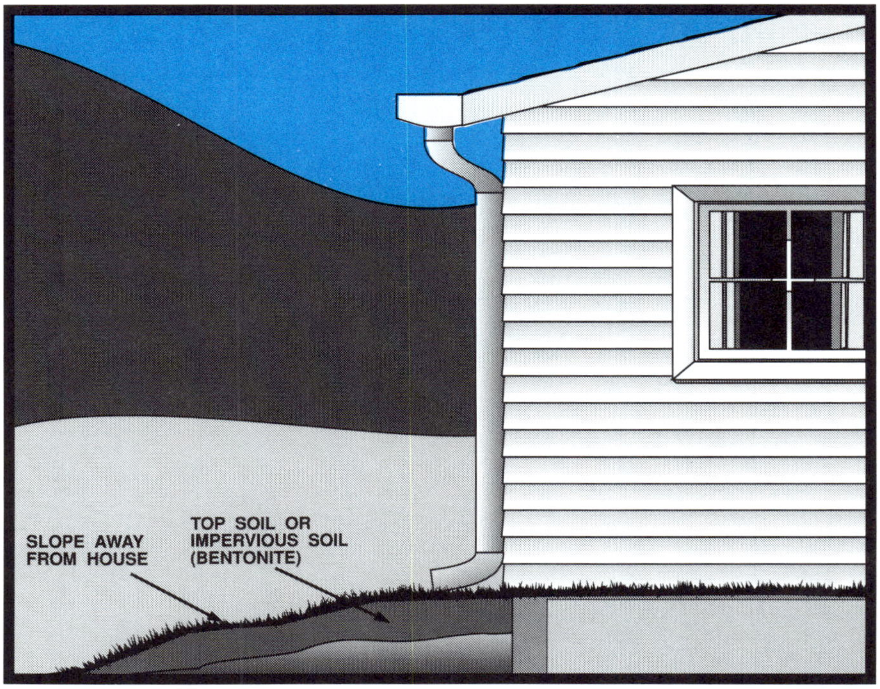

FIGURE 31

SLOPE GRADE AROUND HOUSE PERIMETER WITH IMPERVIOUS TOP LAYER OF SOIL

(SOLUTION D)

SOLUTION

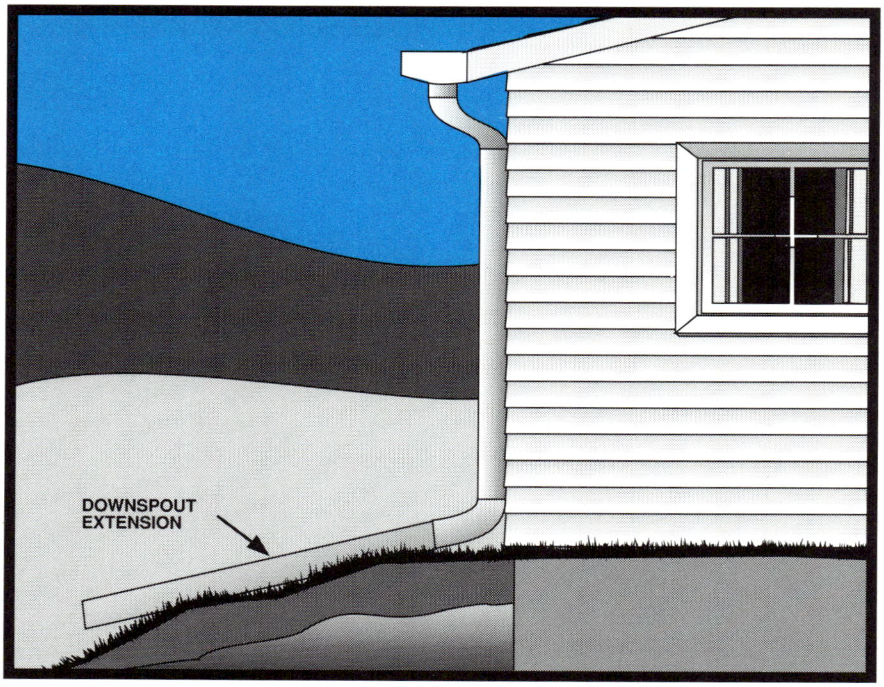

FIGURE 32

EAVESTROUGH AND DOWNSPOUT WITH EXTENSION

(SOLUTION E)

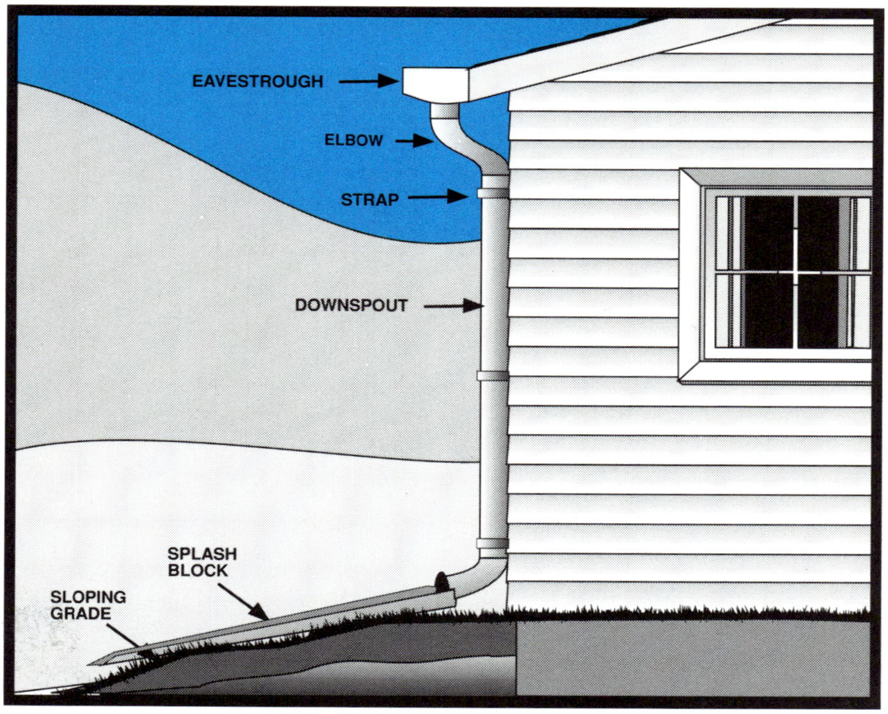

FIGURE 33

EAVESTROUGH AND DOWNSPOUT WITH SPLASH BLOCK

(SOLUTION E)

SOLUTION

E. REPAIR, ADD OR REDIRECT EAVESTROUGHS AND DOWNSPOUTS

DESCRIPTION

- *Eavestroughs* should be pitched towards *downspouts* and be kept free of debris, leaves and twigs.
- Coarse screens over the *eavestroughs* help keep out leaves and loose debris, and are especially useful next to deciduous trees.
- *Downspout/ eavestroughs* connections and *downspout* elbow connections should be sound and unclogged.
- Straps should be provided for *downspouts* so that their position can remain fixed and joints can remain intact.
- *Downspouts* should be drained away from the house, preferably with *downspout* extensions. (See Figure 32.)
- A concrete ground *gutter*, or splash block, can also carry water away from the point of discharge to prevent water pooling and the deterioration of *grade* below that point. Splash blocks are sloped away from the house, with their edges flush with *grade*. (See Figure 33).
- *Downspout* systems designed to drain roof water to the *footing drain* (weeping tile) should be avoided for two reasons. First, if the weeping tile diameter is inadequate, back-up of water and flooding can result. Second, if the below *grade* portion of the *downspout* is later disconnected or broken, it can cause back-up of water and flooding.

LOW TO MEDIUM COST

F. RETROFIT AND INSULATE EXTERIOR BASEMENT WALLS

DESCRIPTION

There are a number of advantages to an exterior basement insulation retrofit, if such a retrofit is possible and feasible. The basement wall temperature is raised and *condensation* of water vapour from either interior or exterior sources can be eliminated. A *vapour barrier* is therefore no longer necessary on the interior surfaces of basement walls. Air leakage can be more easily controlled when exterior insulation is carried past the level of *headers*. Certain types of rigid exterior insulation (draining insulation) can direct any sub-surface water to *footing drains* before it leaks through or saturates the basement walls. Such draining insulation also creates a capillary break and reduces *hydrostatic pressure* against the walls.

Ideally, an exterior basement insulation retrofit (see Figure 34) will include:

- A *dampproofing* coating or *waterproofing* membrane on the exterior surfaces of basement walls (see Solution F-1);
- A permeable drainage board, if the exterior basement walls are not to be insulated or, preferably, draining insulation boards to direct water to the footing drainage system (see Solution F-2);
- The repair of existing or the addition of new *footing drains* and filter cloth over drains; and draining *backfill* (see Solution F-2);
- The installation of exterior rigid insulation. Extruded polystyrene is more durable than expanded polystyrene, urethane or isocyanurate boards. Unidirectional fibreglass insulation boards can provide a drainage layer (capillary break) adjacent to the *foundation walls*;
- Establishing a *grade* away from basement walls (see Solution D).

SOLUTION

PARTIAL INSULATION

In retrofit situations, where the subgrade conditions (such as the type of *backfill* material and the existence and extent of foundation drainage) are unknown, installation of partial and sloped exterior insulation (not the draining type) that allows for good drainage away from the *foundation wall* is possible. (See Figure 35.)

HIGH COST

Excavation and exterior insulation retrofit is a major cost. However, exterior insulation should be installed if the *foundation wall* is ever excavated to repair, replace or install *footing drainage* because insulation represents a low additional cost if excavation has already been done. Such insulation is usually not cost-effective if excavation is done only for the purpose of insulating since excavation is the major cost.

SOLUTION

F-1. PROVIDE EXTERIOR MOISTURE PROTECTION

DESCRIPTION

- Exterior *dampproofing* (mainly to prevent *capillary flow* and the passage of water vapour) is adequate if the site soil and *backfill* are well drained. *Dampproofing* prevents the wetting of wall materials, thereby preventing *capillarity* and slowing vapour *diffusion*.
- Exterior *waterproofing* (to prevent the passage of liquid water under pressure) is recommended if the basement is to be used as a living space. *Waterproofing* resists flow of liquid water (but seldom works for extended periods if the hydrostatic head is high or remains for more than a few days a year).
- Exterior moisture protection is applied up to ground level only to allow for evaporation of any moisture from within the walls.
- Acceptable exterior *dampproofing*:
  - Parging or plastering (120 mm thick coat) with Portland cement and sand mix, or Type M mortar.
  - Cement grout coats, consisting of equal parts of Portland cement and fine sand mixed with water.
  - Asphalt coatings, which can be sprayed, brushed or trowelled, and applied hot or cold. Such coatings are often applied above parging or cement grout coatings.
- Acceptable exterior *waterproofing*:
  - Composite sheet membranes, which include sheets of polyethylene (PE), polyvinylchloride (PVC) or glass fabric coated with rubberized asphalt.
  - Synthetic-rubber sheet membranes.
  - Surface-bonding materials, combining glass fibres with Portland cement and other additives.
- All coatings and membranes should conform to the appropriate requirements of the Canadian General Standards Board (CGSB).

HIGH COST

F-2. REPAIR/REPLACE FOOTING DRAINAGE SYSTEM

DESCRIPTION

The purpose of *footing drainage* is to maintain the sub-surface or ground-water level well below the level of the basement floor.

- Soils ideal for natural drainage include free-draining sands and gravel. These are the preferred material for *backfill*. Backfilling should be done in several layers to minimize the risk of damage to coatings, walls and insulation.

- Older *footing drains* consisted of 100 mm clay tile (drain/*weeping tile*), with joints between tiles slightly open. Today, perforated plastic pipes are used. Plastic pipes withstand soil pressure and action of tree roots better, are laid in continuous lines and do not require the treatment needed for clay tiles.

- *Footing drains* are embedded in, and covered with, at least 150 mm of gravel or crushed stone, and covered with filter cloth. Gravel extension to the top of the fill is prohibitively expensive. Therefore, the gravel covered drains must be protected with filter cloth.

- *Footing drains* are laid horizontally, level and parallel with the bottom of the excavation; as low as, but not lower than, the bottom of footings so as not to undermine the *foundation walls*.

- As mentioned above, after covering the drains with gravel, a filter is placed on top. Filters include filter fabrics (cloth), roofing felts or fibreglass batt insulation.

- Since ideal soils for *backfill* may be expensive, a number of drainage materials can be used, at added cost, to control water adjacent to the *foundation walls*. These systems are connected to the *footing drain* and include:

  - A narrow band of gravel against the *foundation wall*.
  - A corrugated or dimpled plastic sheet, placed against the *foundation wall* to form a drainage cavity between the wall and soil.

SOLUTION

- Special rigid glass-fibre insulation, with the fibre direction parallel and vertical to the *foundation walls*. This insulation is self-filtering and provides an insulating and draining layer against the *foundation walls*.

HIGH COST

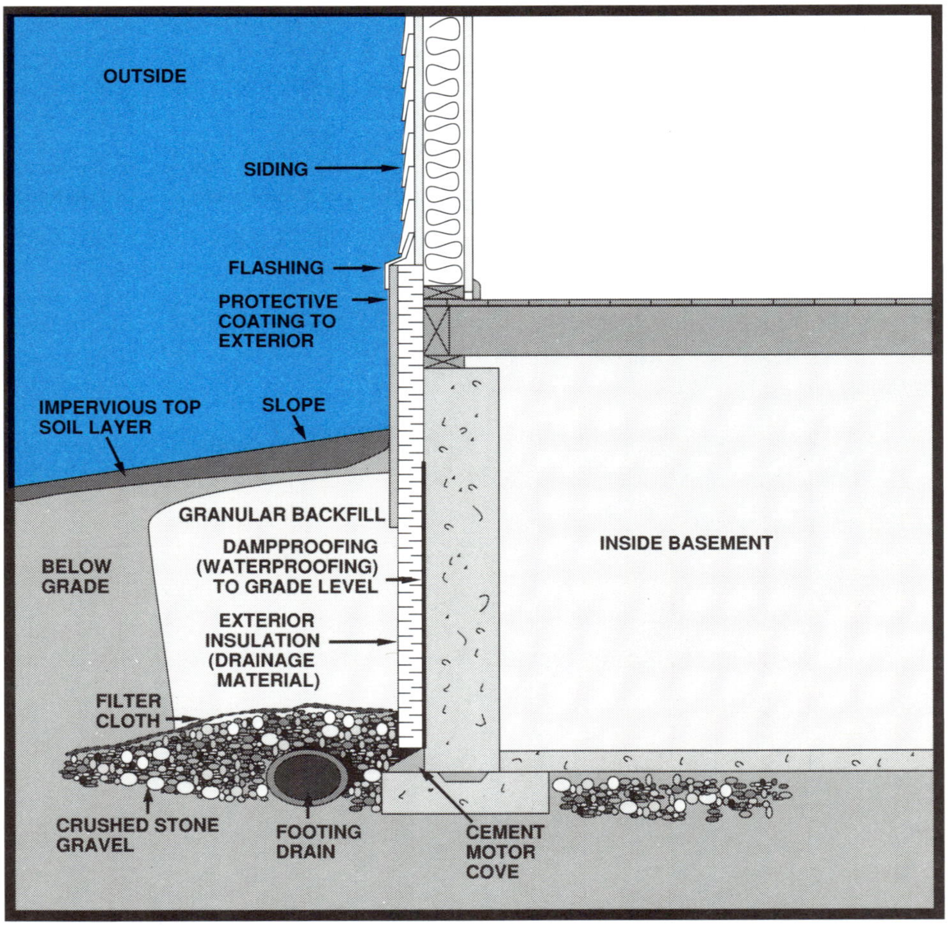

FIGURE 34

EXTERIOR BASEMENT INSULATION

SOLUTION

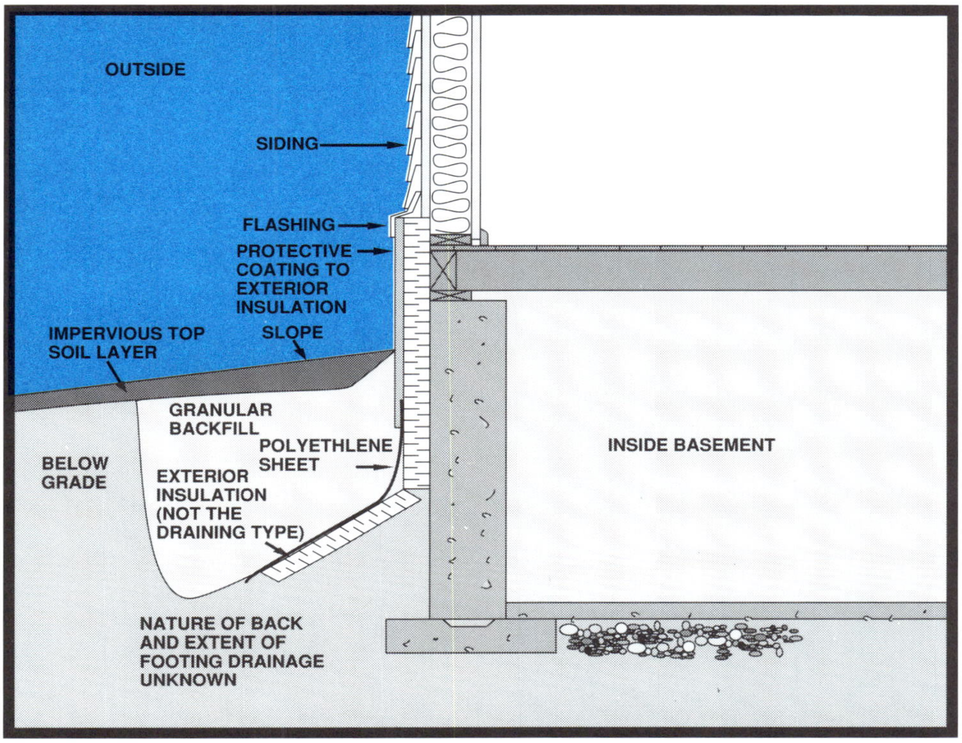

FIGURE 35

PARTIAL EXTERIOR BASEMENT INSULATION

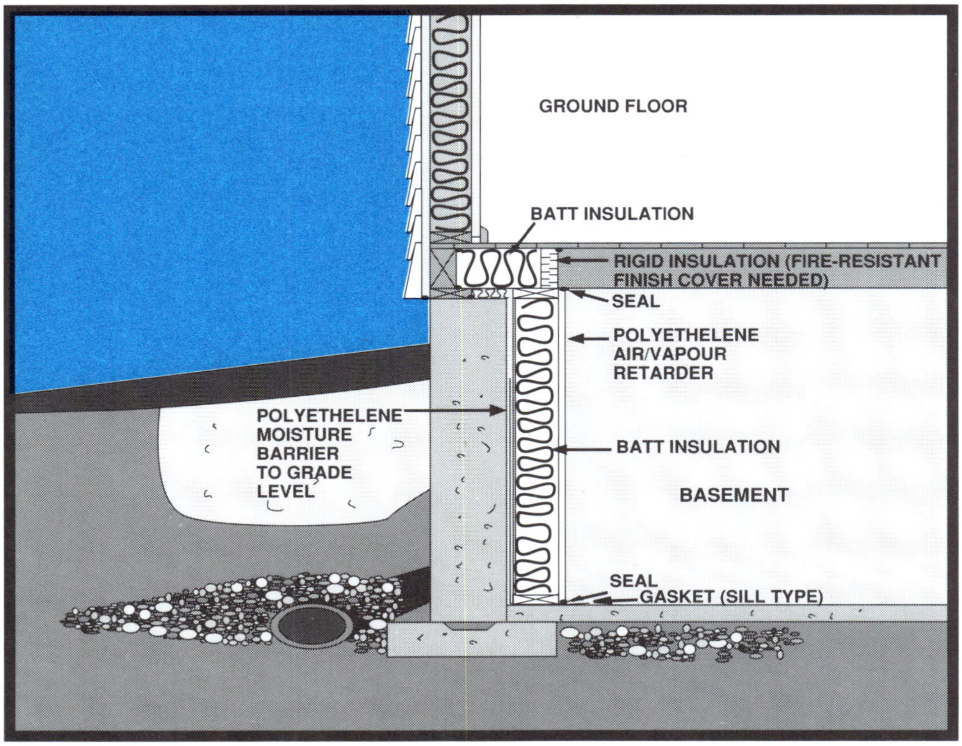

FIGURE 36

INTERIOR INSULATION (FRAME-WALL AND BATT INSULATION)

SOLUTION

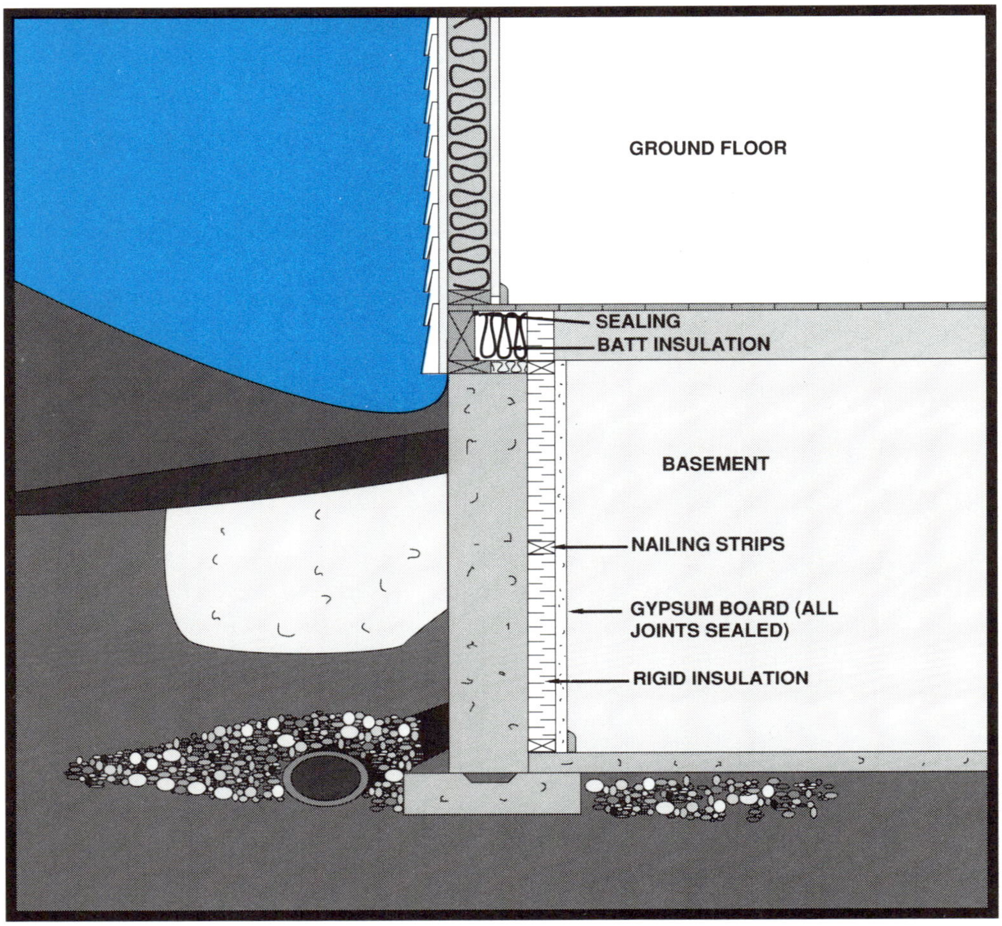

FIGURE 37

INTERIOR INSULATION (RIGID INSULATION AND SEALED GYPSUM-BOARD FINISH)

G. RETROFIT AND INSULATE INTERIOR BASEMENT WALLS AND RETROFIT AIR/VAPOUR RETARDER

DESCRIPTION

Interior insulation reduces heat loss and raises the interior wall surface temperature, minimizing the risk of summer *condensation*. The wall outside of the insulation is, however, colder than it would be if insulation were not applied. Water vapour from the interior must, therefore, be kept from reaching the insulated cavity by a *vapour retarder* and an *air barrier*. This *air barrier* must be tight to prevent moist air carrying water vapour into the cavity.

- One method of interior basement insulation is to install a new wood-frame wall with batt insulation. A moisture barrier is provided to the inside face of the basement wall, but only up to *grade* level. The moisture barrier restricts water vapour *diffusion* from the *foundation wall*. A *vapour retarder* (which can act as *air barrier* if properly sealed) is provided on the warm side of the insulation underneath any finishes. Finishes which are properly sealed can also act as an *air barrier*. (See Figure 36.)
- Another method is to install rigid (board) insulation, with prefabricated metal channels to hold boards, plus a fire-resistant finish material on top. Proper sealing is still required to ensure that air cannot circulate between the board and the wall. (See Figure 37.)
- Partially or poorly insulated basement walls can increase the risk of freeze/thaw damage within the walls.

MEDIUM COST

This method is usually cheaper than exterior insulation and can be done one wall at a time. If it is not done well, however, it may lead to long-term moisture damage within the insulated cavity.

SOLUTION

H. REPAIR STORM DRAINAGE SYSTEM

DESCRIPTION

Consult your local building department officials to determine the extent of your responsibility for any repairs, especially outside your lot. The process, in general, is similar to that described in Solution F-2.

MEDIUM COST

I. REMOVE AND/OR CONTROL INTERNAL/OCCUPANT SOURCES

DESCRIPTION

Based on the internal/occupant sources and causes discussed in Section 2.2, the following solutions are recommended.

- Vent the clothes dryer to the outside or fix the dryer vent. Harmful chemicals can be released when anti-static chemicals are used in a dryer, so they must be vented outdoors.
- Remove damp materials such as firewood.
- Install *ventilation* for basement bathrooms.
- Avoid line drying of clothes in the basement.
- Have a heating technician deal with a poorly drafting furnace and vent any fuel-burning heaters[1].
- Remove humidifiers from basement, including any furnace humidifiers.
- Fix leaking cooling or heating system.
- Control frequency of floor mopping.
- Reduce use of whirlpools and hot tubs, and remove house plants.
- Allow new basement to dry (one year) prior to finishing it, by providing extra *ventilation* when it is cool or cold outside.

---

1 Do not tamper with any fuel-burning equipment. Call an expert!

SOLUTION

J. RETROFIT BASEMENT FLOOR WITH VAPOUR RETARDER

DESCRIPTION

- A polyethylene sheet could be placed under carpets or on any crawl-space floor (split-level house) adjacent to the basement. Protect this sheet from damage by covering it with an appropriate material. Ballast (50 mm of gravel or concrete) may be needed to keep the polyethylene sheet in place.
- The floor could also be insulated as part of a retrofit, with parallel installation of a moisture and air/*vapour retarder*. (See Figure 38.) Care must be taken when installing the air/*vapour retarder* to avoid leakage into the insulated cavity, which could cause moisture damage.

LOW TO MEDIUM COST

SOLUTION

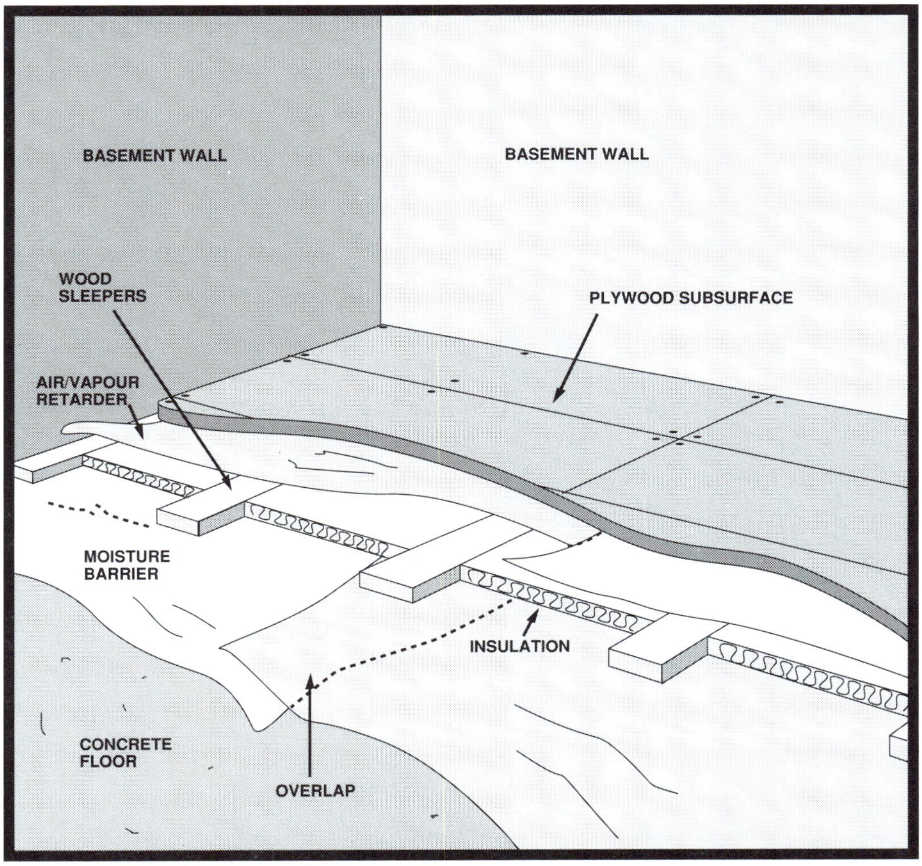

FIGURE 38

RETROFIT BASEMENT FLOOR WITH MOISTURE AND AIR/VAPOUR RETARDER AND OPTIONAL INSULATION

SOLUTIONS

SOLUTION

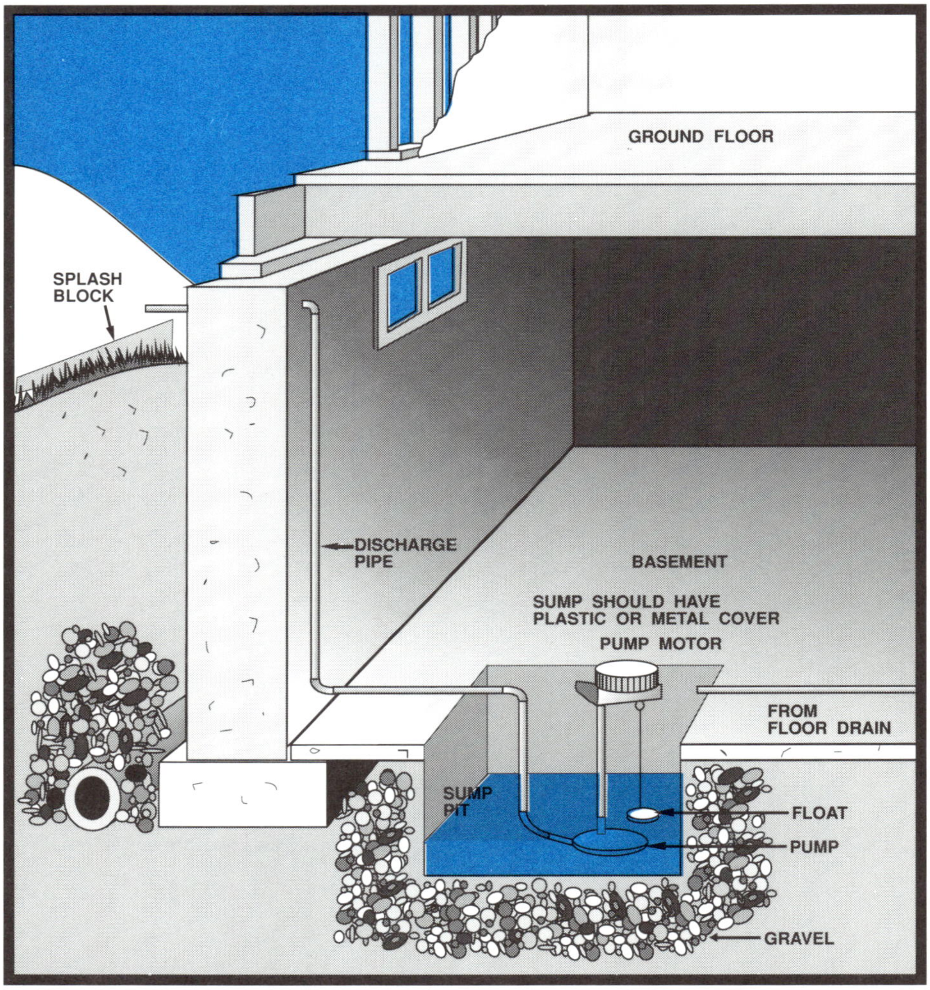

FIGURE 39

INSTALL SUMP TO DEAL WITH PROBLEMATIC WATER LEAKAGE

SOLUTION

K. INSTALL SUMP PUMP

DESCRIPTION

The purpose of the sump pump is to lower the ground *water table* to a height which is below the basement footing and floor level. It is used where the perimeter drain cannot be connected to a storm sewer.

- A sump (pit) should be located at the wettest or lowest area in the basement. The sump should be lined with concrete, metal or large draintile to prevent caving in of the sides. Holes must be provided in the lining to admit ground water. Care should be taken to prevent fine soil particles from being carried to the sump and out with the sump pump. This may require wrapping the sump pit sides and bottom with filter cloth when fine grained soils are encountered. Otherwise, the floor slab and the footings can become undermined. The size of the sump is usually specified by the manufacturer of the pump used. The base of the sump can consist of a 150 mm layer of crushed stone. (See Figure 39.) If the discharge pipe is not connected to a storm sewer or floor drain but drains to the exterior, care must be taken to avoid winter freezing.

- Sump pumps are generally small and compact units which can be automatically or manually operated. If correctly installed according to manufacturers' directions, little maintenance is required. Dirt and lint should be kept out of the sump to avoid clogging. An automatic float or a pressure-activated pump will operate when the water in the sump reaches a level several centimetres below the bottom of the floor slab.

- In most areas, sumps should be covered and vented to outdoors. The only exceptions are areas where the sump is dry for all but a few days of the year and it has been proven that the soil gas carries no *radon* or other dangerous gases.

MEDIUM COST

SOLUTION

L. CONNECT FOOTING DRAINAGE TO WATER TABLE AT KEY POINTS

DESCRIPTION

In the case of a persistent high *water table* and the impracticality of repairing the entire *footing drainage* and *backfill* area, *footing drainage* can be connected to the surface at key points along the *foundation wall*. The systems and materials used to provide drainage at key points have been described in the solution regarding repair of *footing drainage* (Solution F-2). This is a partial solution that does not require excavation all around the house but only in selected areas. It provides a few drainage paths to the *footing draining* system, around the house perimeter, to help lower the *water table*.

MEDIUM COST

M. INSTALL INTERIOR GUTTER SYSTEM DESCRIPTION

If the source and cause of water leakage through basement walls cannot be easily or economically controlled, then the leaking water can be collected in interior *gutter* systems and connected to the floor drain or sump pump. These systems consist of enclosed baseboard *gutters* which are glued and caulked to the floor along the bottom of the basement wall. Some systems just trap leaking water from the base of the wall and channel it away to the drain or sump pump. Other systems can catch and drain away moisture that enters the walls from above the *gutter* system. The interior *gutter* system must be carefully designed and constructed. (See Figure 40.)

In areas where soil gases contain *radon*, methane or excessive water vapour (warm soil next to uninsulated walls and floors), provision must be made to vent collected soil gases to the outdoors. The *gutter* then performs double duty. A poor second choice is to seal all leaks that could vent into the indoor air.

MEDIUM COST

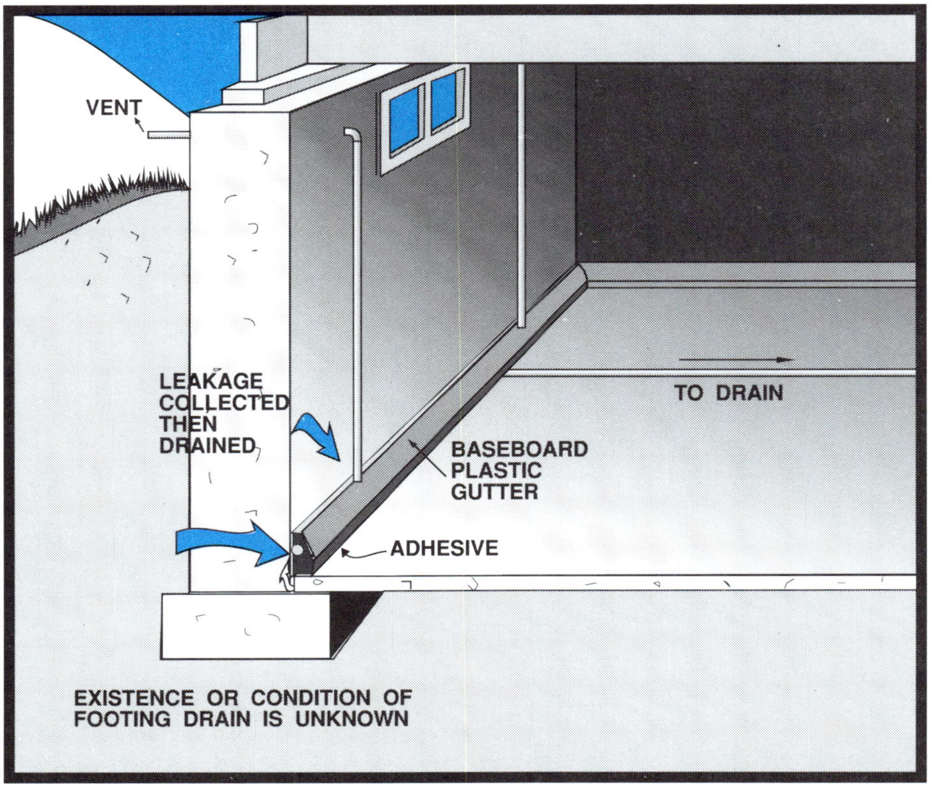

FIGURE 40

INTERIOR GUTTER SYSTEM

SOLUTION

N. UPGRADE WINDOW WELLS

DESCRIPTION

- Windows, or parts of windows, that are below *grade* should be protected by metal or masonry window wells. The bottom of the well should contain gravel to permit good drainage towards the *footing drain*, and to prevent pooling and moisture sources adjacent to the basement *foundation wall*. Walls of window wells are usually made of galvanized corrugated sheet metal.
- Surface run-off should be directed away from the window well.
- If the *backfill* below the well does not drain well, then the bottom of the well can be connected to a *footing drain* via a 150 mm diameter column of crushed stone or gravel wrapped in filter cloth or a strip of glass fibre insulation. (See Figure 41.) Perforated *footing drain* pipe is often used to encase this gravel column.

MEDIUM COST

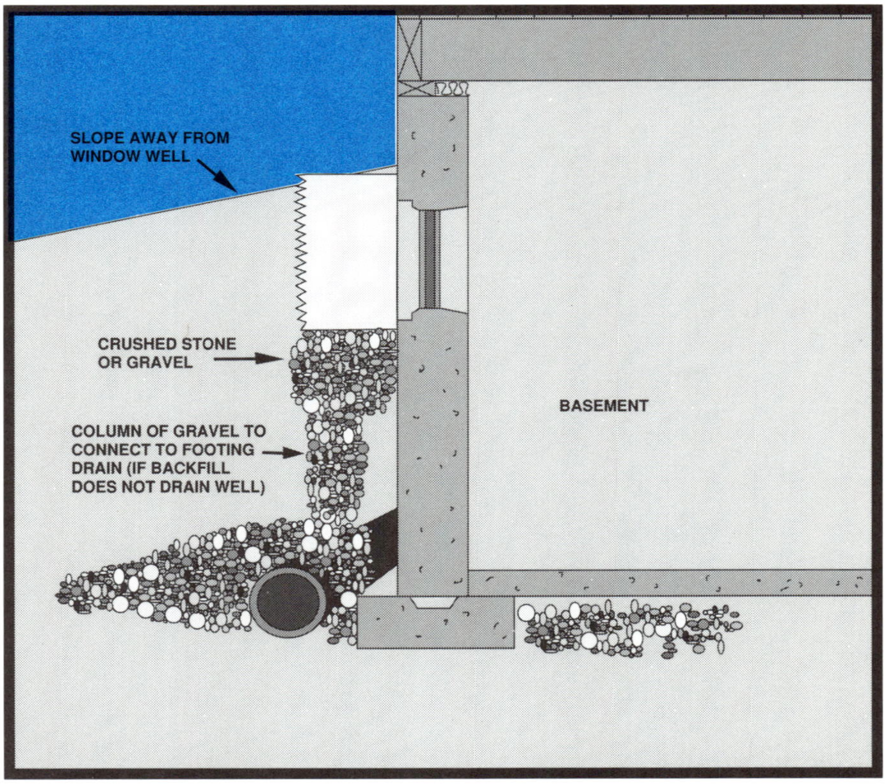

FIGURE 41

UPGRADING WINDOW WELLS

SOLUTION

O. INSTALL INTERIOR FOOTING DRAIN

DESCRIPTION

If it is not possible or practical to excavate around the exterior of the basement walls in order to control water leakage, an interior *footing drain* can be installed and connected to a drainage outlet or sump pump.

- An interior trench along the inside bottom of the footing must be excavated. Another interior trench, connecting to the drainage outlet or sump area, must also be excavated. Drain or weeping tile*s* should be laid. Holes must be drilled through the bottom of the *foundation walls* to relieve outside water pressure and lead that water to the interior drain. The trench and weepholes through the walls should be covered with gravel and topped with concrete. (See Figure 42.)

- A specialty membrane, along the interior of *foundation walls* and connected to the new interior *footing drain*, can also be installed, eliminating the need to drill holes through the *foundation wall*. (See Figure 43.)

- Interior *footing drains* must be carefully designed and built. You must use the services of professional designers and experienced contractors.

- Undermining of the foundations is a possibility when silty soils underlie the footings. *Footing drains* should preferably be wrapped with a filter cloth to prevent serious problems with wall cracking after the footings are undermined.

HIGH COST

SOLUTION

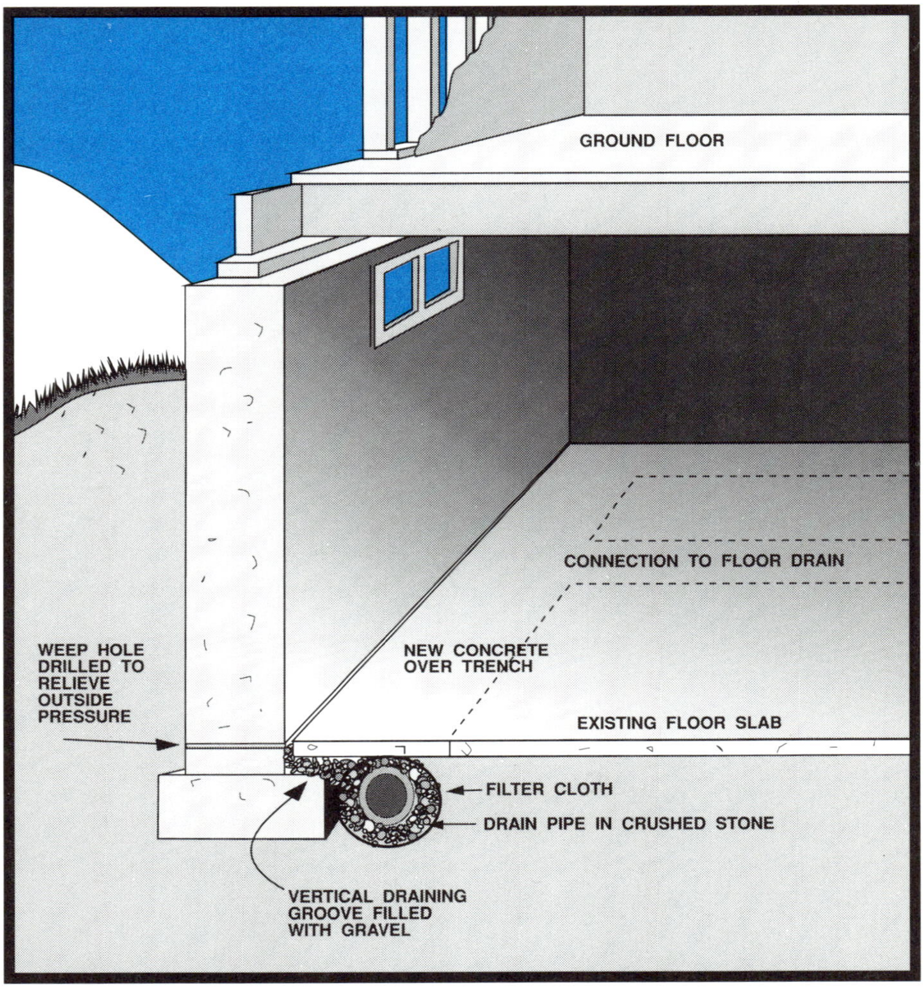

FIGURE 42

INSTALLATION OF INTERIOR FOOTING DRAIN WITH WEEPHOLES TO THE OUTSIDE TO RELIEVE WATER PRESSURE ON FOUNDATION WALL

SOLUTION

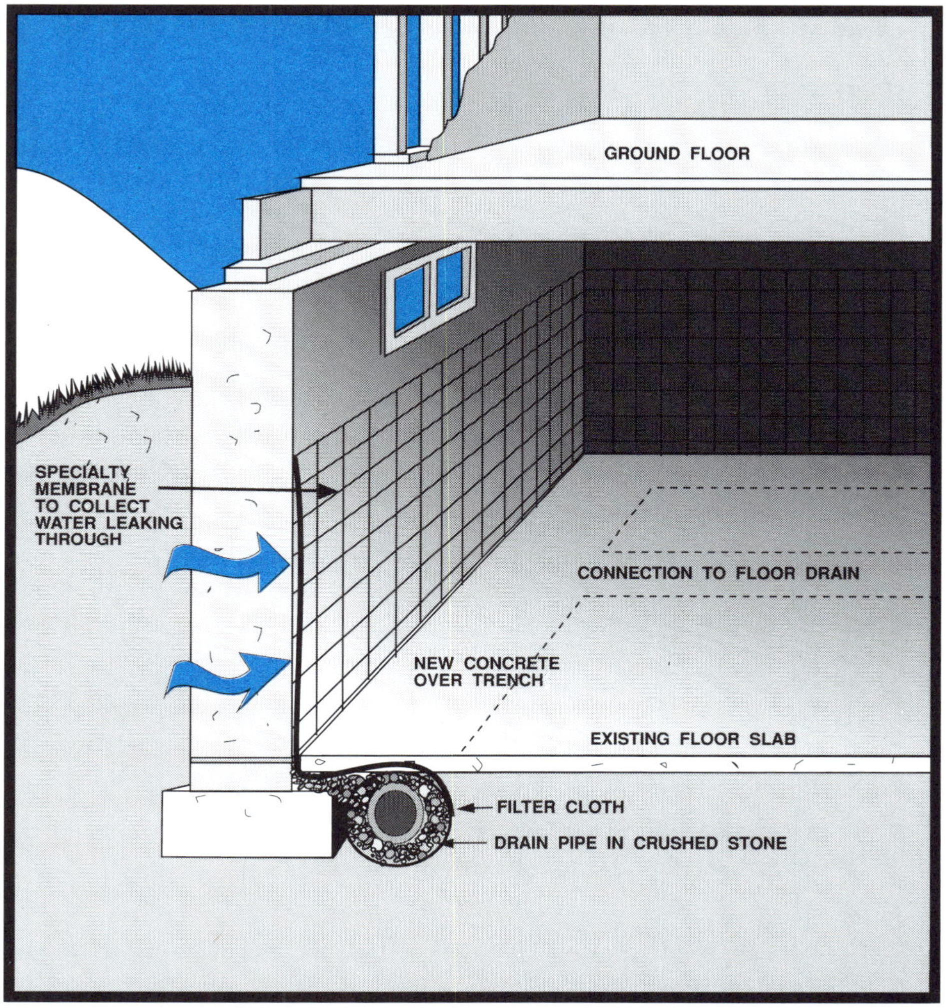

FIGURE 43

INSTALLATION OF INTERIOR FOOTING DRAIN WITH SPECIALITY MEMBRANE TO COLLECT LEAKAGE FROM OUTSIDE

SOLUTION

P. WATERPROOF/DAMPPROOF INTERIOR BASEMENT WALLS

DESCRIPTION

Interior *waterproofing/dampproofing* coatings are usually called for when walls/floors are damp. These coatings will not withstand major *hydrostatic pressure* but will prevent the penetration of water vapour and liquid water under low *hydrostatic pressure*. The major problem with coatings is that they tend to peel off the wall as a result of water and salt build-up behind the wall. Coatings should be applied up to grade-level only, to allow evaporation of any trapped moisture within the wall. Coatings include:

- Epoxy paints, which are either water- or petroleum-based and are mixed from two components prior to use. Epoxy paints, especially water-based, are the best overall performers.
- Ready-mixed, cement-based coatings, which are based on synthetic resins and portland cement mixed in a solvent. These coatings are readily available to homeowners and usually have acceptable performance.
- Cement-based dry powders, which are mixed with water or with pre-packaged liquids before application. These coatings are generally acceptable.
- All materials should conform to the applicable requirements of the Canadian General Standards Board (CGSB).

NOTE:
These coatings work only in cases where the water cannot build up to form a high hydrostatic head behind the wall, and often only for a few years. If water sometimes leaks out in jets or streams, these coatings are not appropriate solutions.

LOW COST

SOLUTION

Q. SEAL AND CONTROL AIR LEAKS

DESCRIPTION

- Air leakage into the basement, especially from the soil around the foundation, should be controlled or preferably eliminated.
- Joints between the floor slab and *foundation walls* should be sealed with caulking. (See Figure 44.)
- Floor drains and sump pits should be provided with tight covers, with a trap primer used for the drain trap. (See Figure 45.)
- Cracks in the floor slab and *foundation walls* should be grouted and sealed. (See Figures 46 and 47.)
- Interior surfaces of block *foundation walls* should be air sealed with *dampproofing* coating, and the top course of concrete block walls should be solid, filled or sealed.
- New approaches to basement design for eliminating air leakage (soil gas), as well as other problems of water and moisture, can also be used. These approaches use a sealed, ventilated and drained cavity, built within the basement enclosure, and can be achieved at modest cost, especially during new construction.

LOW COST

(Sealed, ventilated and drained cavity is sometimes a moderate- or high-cost solution for existing homes.)

SOLUTIONS

SOLUTION

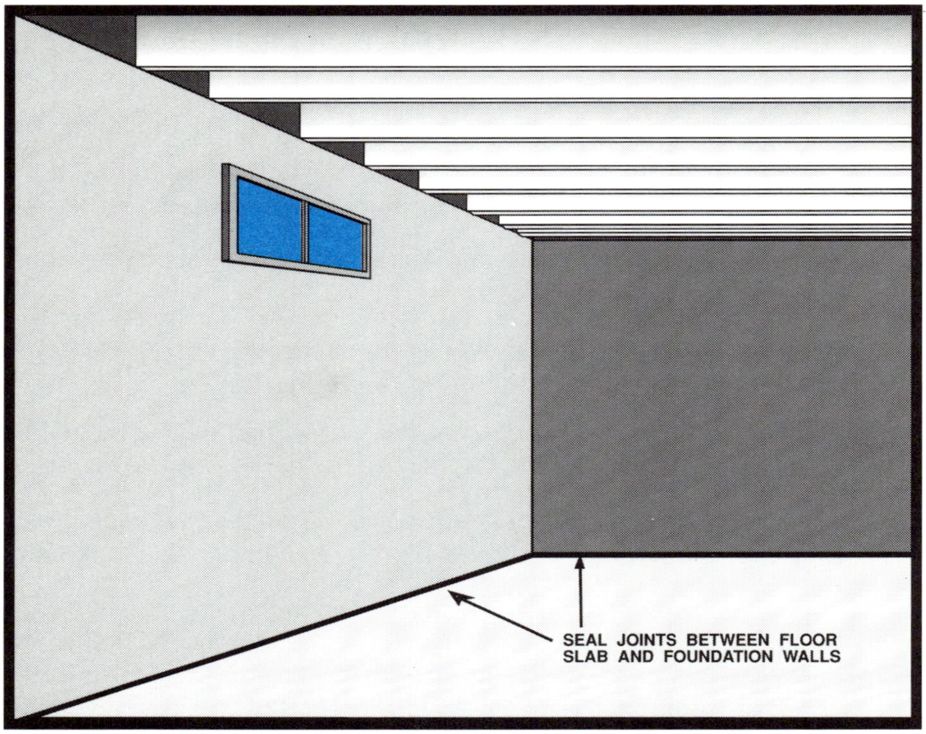

FIGURE 44

SEALING AND CONTROLLING OF AIR LEAKS (BELOW GRADE)

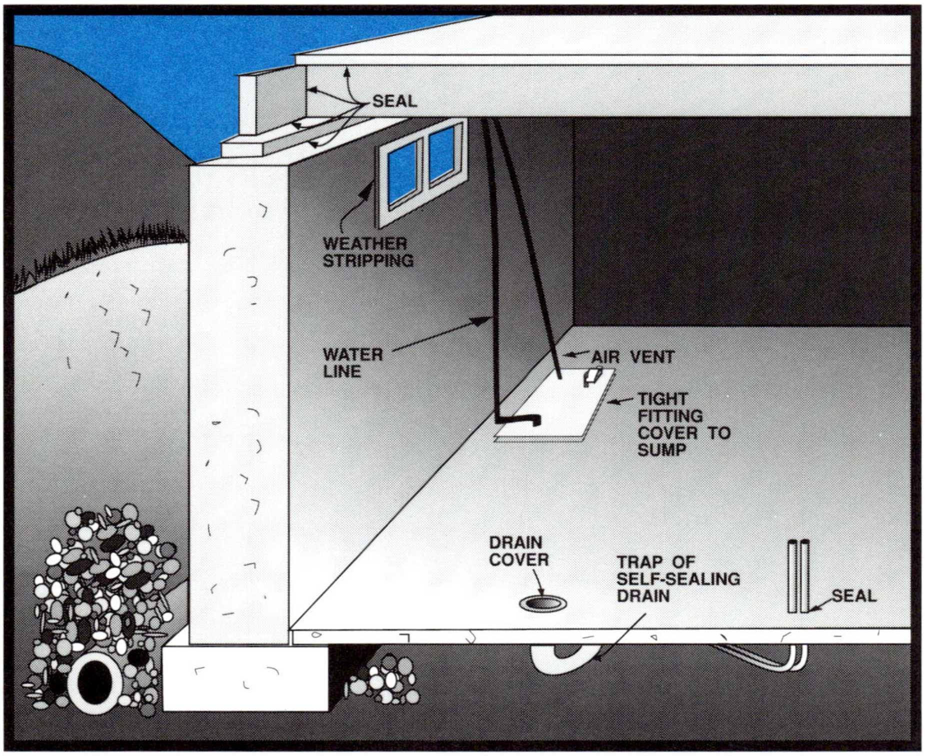

FIGURE 45

SEAL OTHER OPENINGS OR POSSIBLE AIR LEAKAGE POINTS

SOLUTION

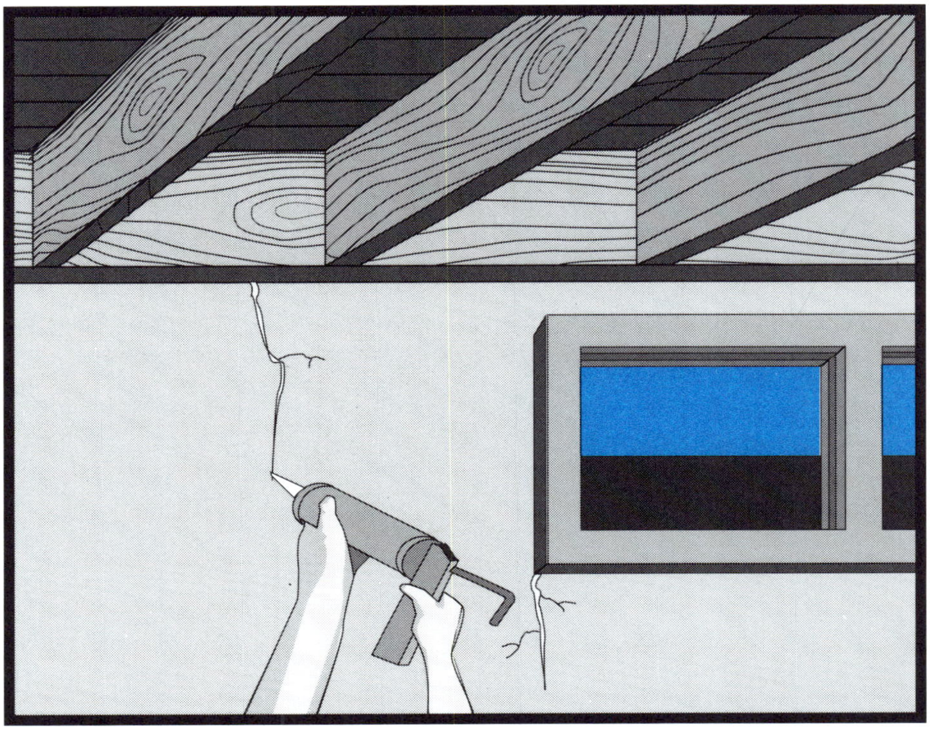

FIGURE 46

SEALING WALL CRACKS

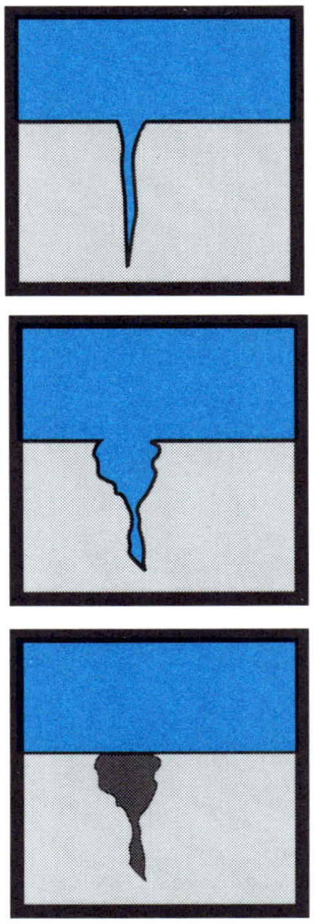

FIGURE 47

CRACK PREPARATION

ORIGINAL CRACK

WIDEN CRACK FOR BETTER ADHESION AND BONDING

SEAL CRACK

SOLUTION

R. CLEAR EXTERIOR HOUSE WALL WEEPHOLES, INSTALL FLASHING

DESCRIPTION

- To avoid rain water draining to the *joist* ends/header area, *flashing* should be installed at the bottom of the exterior wall air cavity.
- Weepholes, where brick finish is used, should be unclogged and kept clear to drain rain water from within the cavity to the outside.
- This solution may not be effective if there are other major moisture sources which connect to the wall cavity.

MEDIUM COST

HOW DID WE DO?

Any comments you have on this guide and its usefulness would be appreciated in order to improve future editions. Please contact CMHC or send comments to:

Investigating, Diagnosing and Treating Your Damp Basement
Canada Mortgage and Housing Corporation
National Office
Research Division
700 Montreal Road
Ottawa, Ontario
K1A 0P7

Appendix A

MATERIAL INFORMATION

Appendix A - Material Information

BATT OR BLANKET INSULATION (INTERIOR USE)

This insulation is easy to install in frame wall cavities and is available in batts or continuous rolls (blankets). Batt or blanket insulation include glass fibre and mineral wool.

RIGID BOARD INSULATION (INTERIOR (EXTERIOR USE)

Rigid board insulations are manufactured from foam polymer materials or glass fibre and are generally more costly than batt or blanket insulation. They have, however, a higher insulating value per unit thickness. If used on the interior, most rigid insulation boards must be covered with a fire-resistant material such as gypsum board. On the above-grade portions of the exterior, boards must be protected from prolonged exposure to sunlight and any solvents.

- **Glass Fibre (Fibreglass) Boards.** In basement applications, a high-density, semi-rigid glass fibre board specifically designed for below-grade, exterior use is recommended due to the drainage properties of its unidirectional structure. Rigid glass fibre is not flammable and does not need protection when used on the interior.
- **Expanded Polystyrene.** Expanded polystyrene is also known as "bead board." High-density versions of these boards can be used on the exterior of foundation walls, while either high- or low-density boards may be used on the interior if protected with a fire-resistant material. Type I, low-density, must *not* be used in contact with soil.
- **Extruded Polystyrene.** Extruded polystyrene contains fine closed cells having a mixture of air and fluorocarbons and is manufactured in high and low densities. It is generally more durable where used as exterior, below-grade insulation than expanded polystyrene, polyurethane and polyisocyanurate boards.
- **Polyurethane and Polyisocyanurate Boards.** Similar to extruded polystyrene, these board have closed cells with fluorocarbons but no air, and usually are double-faced with foil. As with other rigid board insulation, they must be covered with a fire-resistant material when used on the inside of the basement.

LOOSE FILL INSULATION

Loose fill insulation, such as blown or poured cellulose fibre, chopped glass fibre, mineral wool (slag and rock wool) and vermiculite (expanded mica material), is *not* appropriate for below-grade application.

Appendix A - Material Information

SEALANTS

Many types of sealants are commercially available.

- **Acoustical Sealants.** Acoustical sealants bond well to most surfaces and especially to concrete, gypsum and metal. They are very durable (20-year life expectancy) and are the best sealants for overlap stapled joints in poly air/vapour retarders.
- **Silicone Sealants.** Silicone sealants are highly durable (over 20-year life expectancy), flexible and all-purpose sealants. They do not, however, bond well to concrete, mortar or to poly air/vapour retarders.
- **Polysulphide Sealants.** Polysulphide sealants are ideal for concrete, masonry and stone when used with the appropriate primer and are very durable (25-year life expectancy).
- **Acrylic Sealants.** Acrylic sealants are good for most sealing purposes, especially for narrow joints. They have a lower life expectancy than other sealants and are not suitable for sealing poly air/vapour retarders.
- **Butyl-Based Sealants.** Butyl-based sealants bond best to metal and masonry but tend to shrink and have a lower life expectancy than other sealants.
- **Urethane Foam Sealants.** Urethane foam sealants are particularly suited for cracks or gaps exceeding 20 mm in width and for rough gaps in and around foundation walls. They are only suitable for interior use and should be covered with a fire-resistant material.

GASKETS

Where caulking may not be suitable, specialty gaskets are used for sealing joints. Polyethylene foam strips (sill gaskets) are used when sealing between horizontal structural joints such as: top of foundation wall/sill plate; sill plate/header; and header/sub-floor. For deep gaps or cracks, a foam backer rod (compressible foam "rope") is used in conjunction with sealants. Where movement is to be expected, such as around plumbing stacks, flexible neoprene gaskets are used. Sheathing tape may be used for sealing seams of polyethylene air/vapour retarder sheets.

Appendix A - Material Information

AIR/VAPOUR RETARDERS (OR BARRIERS)

The effectiveness of vapour retarders is measured in perm rating (the lower the perm, the more effective the barrier).

- **Polyethylene Sheeting.** For air barrier use, polyethylene sheets should be at least 0.15 mm (6 mil) thick and made from new material conforming to the Canadian General Standards Board (CAN/CGSB-51.34-M86). Polyethylene sheets can function as air/vapour retarders if properly supported on both sides.
- **Rigid Materials.** Most rigid or solid building materials, including rigid insulation foam boards, can serve as air barriers. This is true if all joints, seams and penetrations are properly sealed with suitable sealants and gaskets. Rigid materials may also act as vapour barriers if used in conjunction with 0.05 mm (2 mil) polyethylene sheets or a vapour retarder paint.

Other vapour retarders include aluminum foil, some paints, vinyl wallpaper and certain types of board insulation.

EAVESTROUGHS (GUTTERS) AND DOWNSPOUTS

Copper eavestroughs (gutters) and downspouts are no longer used because of high costs. Today, eavestroughs and downspouts are made of aluminum, galvanized steel or solid vinyl.

- **Prepainted Aluminum.** Inexpensive, rustproof, but very soft to support weights (ladder, for example).
- **Galvanized Steel.** Strong, durable (with factory-applied finish), difficult to paint if not properly prepared with primer.
- **Vinyl.** More durable than either aluminum or galvanized steel, but more expensive; not a large selection of colours.

PROTECTIVE COVERS FOR EXTERIOR INSULATION ABOVE GRADE

Protective covers for exterior rigid-insulation boards above grade, include: asbestos board; pressure-treated plywood; galvanized-metal lath with a parge coating; rigid-vinyl sheeting; painted-metal sheeting; aluminum sheeting; fibre-reinforced, polymer-modified Portland cement; vinyl- acrylic coating; fibre-reinforced plastic sheet; composite protective coating, laminated to insulation; and parging on lath.

Appendix A - Material Information

EXTERIOR BASEMENT INSULATION FLASHING

Flashing for exterior basement insulation and for draining out water from within wall cavities includes galvanized steel (0.33 mm) or zinc. Wood is sometimes used for retrofiting situations.

DAMPPROOFING / WATERPROOFING FOR INTERIOR BASEMENT WALLS

A wide variety of materials are available for interior dampproofing/ waterproofing:

- **Epoxy paints** are mixed from two components, usually the epoxy polymer and a hardener. Epoxy paints are petroleum- or water-based and are generally *very good* for interior dampproofing and waterproofing applications.
- **Ready-mixed, cement-based paints** consist of Portland cement mixed with a synthetic resin and solvent. They are commonly available and are generally *good* for interior dampproofing and waterproofing.
- **Dry, cement-based powders** are also available and are applied after mixing with water or packaged liquid ingredients. These are generally *acceptable* for waterproofing and dampproofing interior applications.
- **Latex-based paints,** which are water-soluble until dry, are generally *unacceptable* for interior basement wall dampproofing and waterproofing.
- **Other products** include rubber paints and acrylic and urethane paints. Water repellents (water seals) are *not* waterproofing products.

EXTERIOR DAMPPROOFING

A choice of materials is available for exterior dampproofing:

- **Parging** is a 12.5 mm coat of Portland cement and sand mix (1:2.5 by volume) or a Type M mortar applied in two 6.25 mm layers. The masonry surface should be cleaned and sprayed with water immediately prior to parging.
- **Cement-grout coatings** consist of Portland cement and fine sand (equal volumes) mixed with water to a thick consistency. Such coatings are applied with a stiff-bristle brush. Two coats are applied, with a 24-hour period between applications.

Appendix A - Material Information

- **Asphalt coatings** can be applied, hot or cold, by spraying, brushing or trowelling (preferred method). They should be applied as per manufacturers' instructions. These coatings are often applied in addition to parging or cement-grout coatings.

- **Dampproofing** is intended to prevent capillary movement of water through bulk materials by preventing wetting of one surface of those materials. It is *not* intended to bridge gaps or to withstand the pressure of a built-up wall of water, such as caused by a high water table and/or a blocked footing drain. It does *not* stop leaks or soil gas flow.

EXTERIOR WATERPROOFING

The following exterior waterproofing materials are available:

- **Composite sheet membranes** are sheets of polyethylene or glass fabric, coated with a rubberized asphalt (1.3 mm thick). Sheets are installed horizontally from the footings upward, with successive overlaps to direct water to the footing drain. A primer is applied to the wall surface prior to installation and all overlaps are sealed.

- **Synthetic-rubber sheet membranes** consist of two or more plies of uniform thickness that are either fully-bonded or laid loose against the exterior masonry wall, according to the manufacturers' instructions. Sheets include butyl rubber, elastomeric EPDM and Neoprene.

- **Surface-bonding materials** combine glass fibres with Portland cement and certain additives and are applied in thin coats (3 mm). For better performance, a bituminous coat (asphalt) is added after curing.

- **Waterproofing** is intended to withstand a moderate head of water pressure, say during a temporarily-high excursion of the water table during spring, but may not continue to stop leaks if the head is high and continuous. A waterproofing layer does stop water and soil gas leaks, at least for short periods of time.

Appendix B

GLOSSARY

Appendix B - Glossary

- **AIR BARRIER:** Material used in the house envelope to retard the passage of air. A good vapour retarder can fulfil both functions and is then called an air-vapour barrier.
- **BACKFILL:** The material used for a trench or around a foundation wall to replace the void left by excavation.
- **CAPILLARY FLOW (CAPILLARITY):** The flow of liquid within small pore passages in a material. This is also called wicking. The water transport mechanism is what allows a sponge to soak up water.
- **CONDENSATION:** The transformation of the vapour content of the air into water on cold surfaces.
- **DAMPPROOFING:** The process of coating the outside of a foundation wall with a special preparation to resist the passage of moisture through the wall. Material used to resist the passage of moisture through concrete floor slabs and from masonry to wood.
- **DECAY FUNGI:** Fungi are parasite plants that prey on plant and animal material, getting their energy indirectly. Fungi are known by their group names: mushrooms, yeasts, moulds and mildews. Fungi grow in materials or on surfaces and can cause problems when a large number of their spores, or parts of the colonies and structures, are breathed in and deposited in the lung.
- **DEW POINT (TEMPERATURE):** The temperature at which a given air/water vapour mixture is saturated with water vapour (i.e., 100% relative humidity). If air is in contact with a surface below this temperature, condensation will form on the surface.
- **DIFFUSION (WATER-VAPOUR DIFFUSION):** The movement of water vapour between two areas caused by a difference in vapour pressure, independent of air movement.
- **DOWNSPOUT:** A pipe which carries water from the eavestrough to the ground or the drainage system.
- **DRAINAGE SWALE:** A small channel that is usually grassed and is wider than deep. It is used for the removal of surface water from a site by natural run-off.

- **DRY ROT:** Decay of timber due to the attack of certain fungi.
- **EAVESTROUGH:** A trough fixed to eaves to collect and carry away the run-off form the roof. Also called gutters.
- **EFFLORESCENCE:** Formation of a white crystalline deposit on the face of masonry walls.
- **FLASHING:** Sheet metal or other material used in roof and wall construction to shed water.
- **FOOTING DRAIN:** Pipe laid in gravel around the footings of a building to drain sub-surface water away from the foundation walls.
- **FOUNDATION WALL:** The lower portion of a structure, usually concrete or masonry, including the footings, which transfers the weight of, and loads on, the structure to the ground.
- **GRADE:** The average level of proposed or finished ground adjoining a building at all exterior walls.
- **GRANULAR MATERIALS:** Granular materials include crushed stone, gravel or certain soils and are used for backfill or under floors to allow for drainage of water towards the footing drains.
- **GUTTER** (See **EAVESTROUGH**)
- **HEADER:** A wood member at right angles to a series of joists or rafters at which the joists or rafters terminate. When used at openings in the floor or roof system, the header supports the joists or rafters and acts as a beam.
- **HYDROSTATIC PRESSURE (HYDROSTATIC HEAD):** Pressure exerted by a build-up of liquid water. It is sometimes expressed as a height or "head" of water which exerts that amount of pressure.
- **IMPERVIOUS MATERIAL:** Soil or other material that will not permit the passage of water.
- **JOIST:** One of a series of horizontal wood members, usually of 50 mm nominal thickness, used for support: thus, floor joist, ceiling joist or roof joist.

- **MILDEW** (See **DECAY FUNGI**)
- **MOULD** (See **DECAY FUNGI**)
- **NAILER (NAILING STRIP):** Usually a strip of wood used to secure panels and allow for nailing of finish materials.
- **PERMEABLE MATERIAL:** Soil or other material that permits the passage of water.
- **ROT** (See **DRY ROT**)
- **R-VALUE:** The overall coefficient of thermal resistance of a building material or assembly.
- **RADON:** An odourless and colourless radioactive gas that can enter a house from the soil beneath and around the house foundation.
- **RELATIVE HUMIDITY:** The percentage of the existing partial pressure of water vapour in a space compared to the saturation pressure at the same temperature; for example, air containing one half the amount of moisture it is capable of holding has a relative humidity of 50 percent.
- **SEALANT:** A flexible material used on the inside (or outside) of a building to seal gaps in the building envelope in order to prevent uncontrolled air infiltration and exfiltration.
- **SILL PLATE:** A structural member anchored to the top of a foundation wall, upon which the floor joists rest.
- **VAPOUR DIFFUSION** (See **DIFFUSION**)
- **VAPOUR RETARDER (BARRIER):** Material (or system) used in the house envelope to retard the passage of water vapour or moisture. The performance is rated in perms.
- **VENTILATION:** The movement of outdoor air through the house's exterior envelope via leaks or intended openings, both inward and outward again. Distribution is the transfer of ventilation air into and out of rooms or other confined spaces inside the house's envelope. Circulation is the movement of air (including a fraction of the ventilation air) within rooms or confined space.

- **WATERPROOFING (WATERPROOF MEMBRANE):** Sheet materials applied to a roof or wall surface to prevent the penetration of water, often in several layers or "plies."
- **WATER TABLE:** The level below which the ground is saturated with water.
- **WEEPING TILE** (See **FOOTING DRAIN**)
- **WICKING ACTION** (See **CAPILLARY FLOW**)

Appendix C

BASEMENT MOISTURE FLOW CHART AND CHECKLIST

Appendix C - Basement Moisture Flow Chart and Checklist

BASEMENT MOISTURE FLOW CHART

This flow chart displays how the basement moisture problem was structured for purposes of preparing this guide. It organizes the main basement moisture sources and causes, resulting symptoms and solutions for treatment. The flow chart should be read from left to right.

The numbers for the sources and causes, symptoms and solutions correspond to those used in the text. Thus, the flow chart helps you understand at a glance the interrelationship of the elements involved in the basement moisture problem.

CHECKLIST

The basement moisture and diagnosis checklist helps record moisture conditions and solutions. It is intended for use by homeowners to structure the investigation of the house currently occupied, and by prospective homebuyers wishing to evaluate the significance of observed moisture problems in any house they are considering buying.

By systematically inspecting the house and recording your findings on the checklist, you can begin to plan and cost the steps needed for correction.

Appendix D

REFERENCES

Appendix D - References

1. Abendroth, H.R. **"A Design Guide for Dry Basements in Existing Homes: Final Report."** Prepared for the U.S. Department of Housing and Urban Design, Office of Policy Development & Research; prepared by AMAF Industries Inc., Washington, D.C. Springfield, Va.: NTIS, 1981.

2. Anon. **"Moisture Protection."** New England Builder - March 1988, p. 44.

3. Canada Mortgage and Housing Corporation (CMHC). **"Condensation in the Home: Where, Why, and What to Do About It."** Ottawa: CMHC, 1980.

4. CMHC. **"A Glossary of House-Building and Site-Development Terms."** Ottawa: CMHC, 1982.

5. CMHC. **"Moisture and Air: Problems and Remedies."** Ottawa: CMHC, 1989.

6. CMHC. **"Moisture Problems."** Builders' Series. Ottawa: CMHC, 1987.

7. Crocker, C.R., **"Moisture and Thermal Considerations in Basement Walls."** Canadian Building Digest No. 161, National Research Council, Ottawa: NRC Division of Building Research, 1974.

8. Energy Efficiency Branch of Alberta Energy. **"Basement Insulation."** Energy Matters Series. Edmonton, Alberta: The Branch, 1990.

9. Energy, Mines and Resources Canada (EMR). **"Keeping the Heat In."** Ottawa: EMR, 1990.

10. de Marne, H. **"Curing the Leaky Foundation."** New England Builder, March 1986, pp. 22-25.

11. National Centre for Appropriate Technology. **"Moisture and Home Energy Conservation: How to Detect, Solve and Avoid Related Problems."** Prepared for the U.S. Dept. of Energy Conservation and Renewable Energy, Small Scale Technology Branch, Washington, D.C. NCAT, 1983.

12. National Research Council, Associate Committee on the National Building Code. **"National Building Code of Canada."** 10th edition. Ottawa: The Council, 1990.

13. Rule, R.H. **"Making Basements Dry."** Home and Garden Bulletin No. 115. Washington: U.S. Dept. of Agriculture, 1970.

14. Sellers, D. **"Waterproofing Your Basement."** Rodale's Practical Homeowner, September 1988, pp. 55-56.

15. Timusk, J. **"Control of Decay and Heat Losses in Basement Walls."** Conference Proceedings: Building Science: Design and Rehabilitation of Building Envelopes, Canadian Society for Civil Engineers, 1982.

16. Timusk, J. **"Insulation Retrofit of Masonry Basements."** Report prepared for the Ontario Ministry of Municipal Affairs and Housing, Toronto, 1981.

17. White, J.H. **"Ventilation for Humidity Control."** A research report. Ottawa: CMHC, 1984.

(4) 16' X 12' $6000

Cedar

Step / Landing

(3) $3000

(2) $1500

(1) $18,500

10,000 cash

459 2355

819

7pm

6pm